RAILWAYS
THE HOLY LAND

Alon Siton

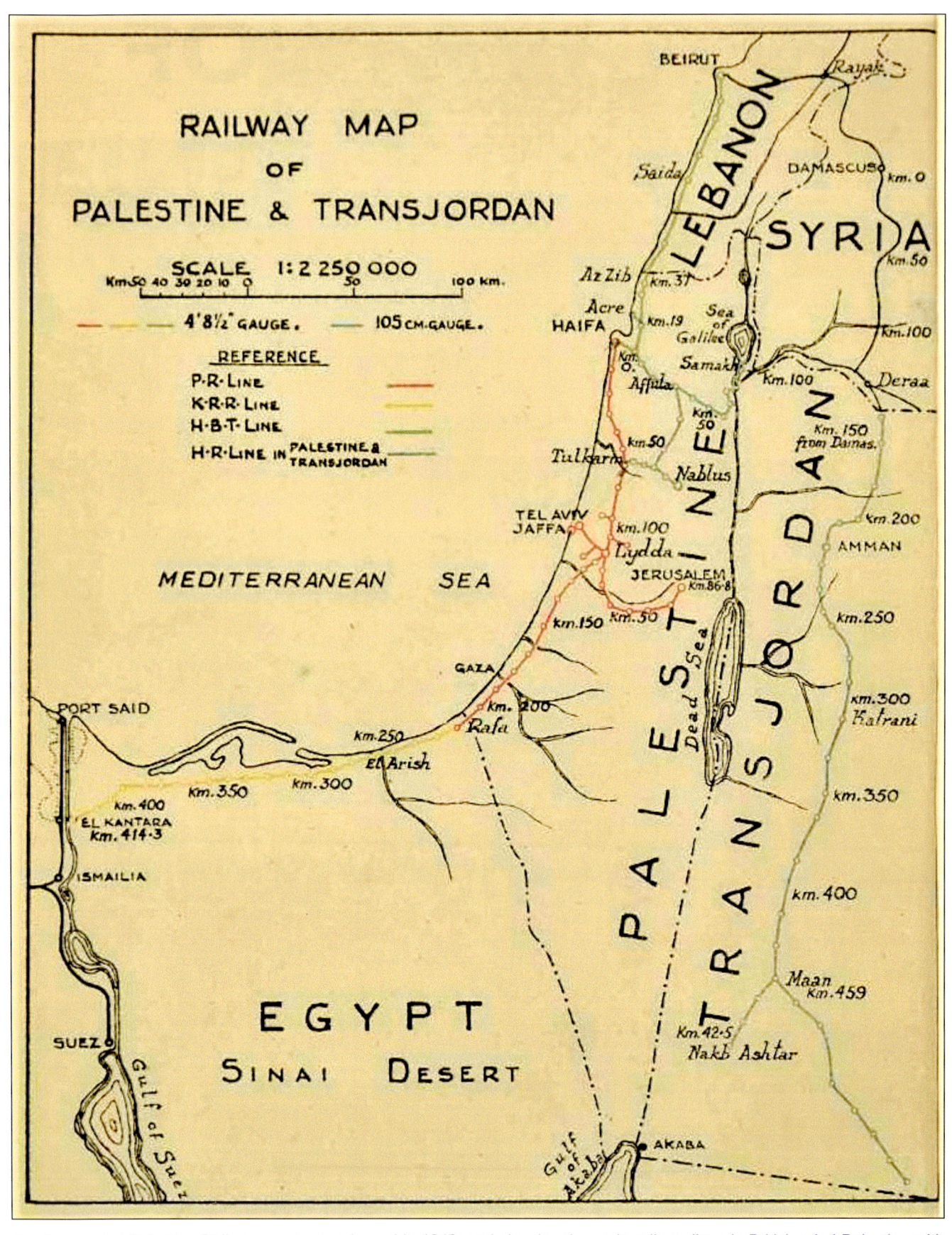

A colour-coded Palestine Railways route map issued in 1946, and showing the main railway lines in British-ruled Palestine with connections to Egypt, Jordan and Lebanon.

HISTORICAL TIMELINE

1517-1917 The Middle East is a part of the Turkish Ottoman Empire

1892 – 26.09 Inauguration of the Jaffa-Jerusalem Railway

1900 – The Hedjaz Railway

1905 – 15.10 Inauguration of the Haifa-Damascus line

1913 – The Hedjaz Railway is extended into the Samaria region

1914-1918 World War I

1917 – 11.12 Jerusalem officially surrenders to General Allenby

1917 – 27.12 First British train reaches Jerusalem

1918 – 19-21.09 The Ottoman Army is defeated in the Battle of Megiddo. The British advance into Damascus and Aleppo

1918 – Completion of the British-built standard gauge line from Sinai to Haifa

1920 – 01.10 Palestine Railways are officially created

1922 – 11.09 The British Mandate of Palestine officially begins

1939-1945 World War II

1941 – 08.06 Britain invades French-ruled Lebanon and Syria

1942 – Construction of a military line from Haifa to Beirut and Tripoli

1945 – 01.11 "Night of the Railways" heavy damage in 153 Jewish underground attacks on railways and rolling stock in British Palestine

1946 – 25.05 Britain grants full sovereignty to the Kingdom of Jordan

1946 – 16.06 "Night of the Bridges" eleven road and railway bridges are destroyed, cutting off the railway lines to Syria, Jordan and Egypt

1946 – 17.06 The railway workshops in Haifa are damaged in a Jewish underground attack, including steam locomotives and equipment

1947 – 29.12 UN Partition Plan of Palestine

1948 – 14-15.05 End of British Mandate in Palestine. The State of Israel is established

1948 – 20.06 First Israeli passenger train in the Haifa metropolitan area

1949 – 07.08 First Israeli passenger train on the Haifa-Tel Aviv-Jerusalem line

1951 – 14.11 Closure of the Hedjaz Railway in Israel

1952 – 12.08 ISR No. 101, Israel's first diesel-electric locomotive, enters service

1953 – 15.04 Inauguration of the new Haifa-Tel Aviv coastal route

1954 – 04.11 Inauguration of the new Tel Aviv Central station

1954 – ISR receives the first batch of new General Motors (EMD) G12 diesel locomotives

1955 – ISR's first modern passenger coaches arrive from Germany

1956 – 29.03 Inauguration of the standard gauge Beersheba railway

1956 – ISR receives twelve Maschinenfabrik Esslingen three-car diesel trains from Germany

1967 – 05.06 The Six Day War. Israel takes over the Sinai Peninsula and Gaza from Egypt, the Judea and Samaria regions from Jordan, and the Golan Heights from Syria

1967 – 02.09 Opening of the Dimona line for passenger traffic

1979 – 26.03 Israel and Egypt sign a peace agreement

1988 – Establishment of the Ports and Railways Authority

1992 – ISR receives new IC3 diesel trains

1993 – Inauguration of the Ayalon River railway in Tel Aviv

1994 – 26.10 Israel and Jordan sign a peace agreement

2001 – The first double-decker coaches arrive in Israel

2015 - Inauguration of the new Western Negev railway

2016 – 16.10 Inauguration of the new Haifa-Bet Shean line

INTRODUCTION

It is justifiably argued that any presence of railways in the Middle East has always been due to political, military and religious reasons, and hardly ever the result of natural economic growth. There is ample evidence to support such a claim, in light of the region's turbulent history over the last century and the undisputed fact that it remains a politically active volcano right down to this day. The Jaffa & Jerusalem Railway of 1892 was originally built to carry Russian pilgrims from the port of Jaffa to the Christian holy sites in Jerusalem, only to end up as a Turkish military line in World War I. The Hedjaz Railway was similarly a combined religious and military undertaking that was initiated by the Turkish Sultan, to carry Muslims to the holy city of Medina in times of peace, and German and Austro-Hungarian troops and military equipment between Damascus in the north and Arabia in the south during the Great War, including a branch line, across the Jordan River, to Beersheba and the Sinai Desert, in preparation of an attack on the Suez Canal. The Baghdad Railway, better known in German as the Bagdadbahn, was celebrated as a triumph of modernity, but was actually a huge strategic asset for the German Empire by creating an alternative overland route for the Suez Canal that would have directly linked the German colonies in Africa and Asia with the Kaiser in Berlin. Ironically, this line was only completed in 1940, long after the end of the war in 1918 and the demise of the Turkish and German Empires. The standard gauge line to Haifa was extended from Egypt alongside the British invasion of Palestine, at first serving hospital and military trains, but no civilian traffic whatsoever. In 1942, that same line was continued up the Mediterranean coastline from Haifa to Beirut and Tripoli, in western Lebanon, again for the benefit of the British war effort in the Middle East. Civilian trains in the Middle East were apparently not a major factor, always giving precedence to international political plans and the ensuing military campaigns.

Upon the Second World War's end, in 1945, the Middle East was already in a transition period that gave birth to a league of Arab-Muslim states in which Israel, the Jewish homeland, still today remains an outsider. The old colonial railway systems were all gone and with them, the international routes linking Africa with Asia and Europe. On the other hand, railway development in the Middle East could now, at least in theory, take a new direction, with each country free to manage and run its railways according to national, rather than imperial, considerations and interests. For the Middle East, this often meant a long period of stagnation and halted development, and in some particularly unfortunate cases, as in Lebanon, the senseless destruction of the railway system in a civil war and no more trains at all. In war-torn Syria as in Jordan, Egypt and Iraq, what little progress that has so far been achieved usually amounts to a short period of post-independence growth, followed by a general decline in living standards and no marked development of the railway system beyond that point. In practical terms, this comes down to the use of diesels, instead and sometimes together with, the older steam locomotives. Israel, that tiny, barely visible dot on the map with a population of nine million inhabitants (as of 2018), is the exception to the generally unpromising situation in most parts of the Middle East. By global standards, the booming Israeli economy is prosperous enough that Israel ranks within the UN Human Development Index Top Twenty Nations as "Very Highly Developed." It has a welfare system, modern infrastructure, and a successful hi-tech market with the second-largest number of startup companies anywhere in the world, after the United States. It therefore comes as no surprise that the Israeli railway system, the successor to the erstwhile Palestine and the western Hedjaz Railways, is enjoying a renaissance of unprecedented proportions. On top of the meteoric rise in passenger traffic since 2000, modern equipment is regularly entering service in Israel and the upgrade from diesel to electric locomotives is in full swing on the new Tel Aviv-Jerusalem high speed line. Short and long-haul lines are added everywhere, including the Haifa-Bet Shean railway, some seventy years after the end of all traffic on that historical route. At the time of writing, ISR is expecting the delivery in 2020 of double-deck electric trains from Siemens (330 coaches in total) that will be added to the existing fleet of 520 passenger coaches. From a humble beginning in 1948, and with nothing more than a handful of steam locomotives and worn-out wooden coaches, the railways of Israel have come a long way and have successfully and outstandingly stood the test of time. On their 75th anniversary, this book is dedicated to their fascinating story, using previously unpublished photos from the author's own private collection.

One final word on politics. The Middle East has been on the top of the news for as long as one can recall, even more so since the creation of the State of Israel in 1948 and Israel's ongoing and seemingly unsolvable territorial and religious dispute with the Palestinians and the Arab world. This book is only and exclusively concerned with the history of the railways in the relatively small but infinitely important area between the Mediterranean Sea in the west and the Jordan River in the east, without making any specific political statements in favour of any of the warring parties. It is not a political analysis of Israeli-Arab relationships, but a nostalgic trip to bygone days in the Middle East when one could board the Orient Express in Paris and travel, via Istanbul and Aleppo, to Jerusalem and Cairo in great comfort, with connections to Baghdad and the Persian Gulf, or down the Nile to Sudan and elsewhere in Africa.

The author wishes to thank the following for their help and support in the making of this book: Iain McCall, Greg Martin, Helmut Dahlhaus, Richard Simon, Laurence Sly, Matan Silberstein, Micha Sender and Chen Melling.

A BRIEF DESCRIPTION OF ISRAEL

Located along the eastern Mediterranean coastline, Israel rests on the historical crossroads between Europe, Asia and Africa. A small country by any measure, and as big as Wales, it shares borders with Lebanon to the north, Syria to the northeast, the Kingdom of Jordan to the east, Egypt to the southwest and finally with the Palestinian territories in Samaria, Judea and the Gaza Strip. The main cities are Tel Aviv, the gateway to Israel and the country's financial and cultural centre; Jerusalem, the proclaimed capital and the seat of the Israeli government; Haifa, overlooking Haifa Bay from the top of Mount Carmel, and Beersheba, a thriving metropolis in the Negev Desert. The northern tip of the Red Sea, in the south of Israel, provides access to the Indian Ocean and the Far East, as well as to a breathtaking underwater nature reserve of tropical fish. The Sea of Galilee, also known as Lake Kinneret, is Israel's main water source, and together with Capernaum, Tabgha and the Jordan River, doubles as the leading site for Christian pilgrims in the Holy Land. For a magnificent panorama of the area, Nazareth and Mount Tabor are a short drive away from the lake and a popular stop for visitors to the north of the country.

Mount Hermon's snow-capped summit and the Golan Heights form Israel's border with Syria. More to the south, the landscape changes into a wide area of cultivated land before reaching the Sea of Galilee and Tiberias. The Jordan Valley is Israel's natural border with the Kingdom of Jordan and stretches out to Jericho and the Dead Sea. The Gulf of Eilat, on the Red Sea, is a three-state border with Jordan and Egypt and a popular destination for sun-starved holidaymakers. The Israeli coastline runs down from western Lebanon to Haifa Bay and Tel Aviv, curving gracefully as it reaches the ports of Ashdod and Ashkelon on the approach to the Gaza Strip. Moving inland, the Negev Desert, from Beersheba to Eilat, occupies half of Israel's total area and has long since been found to be ideal for growing the finest dates, watermelons and bell peppers. Jerusalem is right at Israel's heart, with Bethlehem and Hebron below and the rolling Samaria hills above it.

What Israel lacks in size, it more than compensates for in content. In the north, the Crusader castles are romantic remnants from Saladin's conquest of the Holy Land in 1187. Jerusalem's Old City is a UNESCO World Heritage Site, as are the Bahai Gardens in Haifa and Akko, ancient Megiddo, the Bauhaus in Tel Aviv and Masada, to name a few examples. Visiting nature reserves is a popular Israeli habit and accordingly, the country is rich with wildlife sanctuaries and archaeological sites. The culinary scene has often been described as "the place where east meets west" and for all of their political differences, both Israelis and Palestinians get to enjoy the most delicious food imaginable.

After changing more hands than one can recall, going from the biblical kingdoms of Assyria and Babylon via the Persian, Roman and Byzantine Empires to the 12th century Crusades and the subsequent Muslim invasion and subjugation of the Holy Land, in 1517 the Middle East came to rest in Turkish hands. The entire area became a part of the Ottoman Empire, under the Sultan's rule in Constantinople or present-day Istanbul. A tiny province of no particular value, the Holy Land lapsed into a coma from which it only recovered when it was suddenly drawn into the centre of European politics. Napoleon's campaign in Egypt and Syria (1798–1801) was meant to interfere with Britain's access to India, and would have probably succeeded had he not run into Commodore Sidney Smith and his Royal Navy flotilla in Akko, who came to the city's rescue. His defeat was Britain's victory in more than the obvious military way. Napoleon's adventures in the Middle East coincided with Europe's colonial expansion into Asia, Africa and South America, and the European powers were eager to gain a solid foothold in western Asia for the usual political reasons. European advisors and consultants were whispering in the Sultan's ear in the race for power in the Middle East, with the result that foreign investments began to pour into the Holy Land. Before long, Italian, Austro-Hungarian and German postal services were introduced in Jerusalem. German agricultural communities, the so-called Templers, were created in Haifa, Jerusalem and elsewhere around the country (although for evangelical reasons and not necessarily as part of Germany's official colonial policy). The European consuls were gaining influence over the local Turkish government officials and would often intervene in Turkish administrative affairs to tip the scales in their favour.

While all this was happening, a 19th century Jewish national awakening led to the establishment of the Zionist movement under Theodor Herzl, a Hungarian Jew who was called to action in the wake of the Alfred Dreyfus outrage and the strong anti-Semitic sentiments in France. Herzl envisioned a sovereign and independent Jewish state, dedicating his entire life to turning the idea into reality. His dream came true in 1947, after thirty years of a British Mandate in Palestine, when the United Nations adopted a partition plan in which the Jews would get a piece of the land where they could have their national home. The plan was accepted by the Jews, and rejected by the Arabs. The following year, Israel was declared an independent state. War broke out at once, with Israel fighting for its life against the heavily armed and properly organized forces of Lebanon, Syria, the British-run Jordanian Legion, Egypt and Iraq. When the war ended, the invading Arab armies were crushed to pieces and Israel had won most of the former British Mandate territory to the west of the Jordan River. The Samaria and Judea regions, and east Jerusalem, were under hostile Jordanian control, and an Egyptian military governor was appointed to oversee the Gaza Strip. In the Six Day War of June 1967, Israel took over the West Bank territories from Jordan and the Sinai Peninsula from Egypt, chasing the Jordanian Legion out of the country and winning also the Golan Heights from Syria. Israel has since then returned Sinai to Egypt in the Egyptian-Israeli peace agreement of 26 March 1979, but continues to hold the West Bank territories for religious and security reasons despite violent Palestinian opposition and international criticism.

HISTORICAL BACKGROUND

Trade routes connecting the Middle East and northern Africa with southwestern Europe and India have been in existence already since biblical times. The Nabatean Incense Trade route, whose commercial centres of Ovdat and Shivta, in Israel's Negev desert, are World Heritage Sites, was a combination of several land and sea routes across Asia, through which precious incense, spices and other luxury goods such as pearls, silk and even gold were carried in camel caravans from Egypt, Mesopotamia and Arabia to the Mediterranean ports, to be shipped away to the markets in Turkey and Greece. The Via Maris (literally "way of the sea") is a historic road that runs from Egypt and up the Mediterranean coastline to the northern Jordan Valley and onwards to Syria, Anatolia and Mesopotamia. In times of peace as in times of war, these ancient and largely unchanged roads remained the only way to move about both in and outside the Holy Land.

The growing European interest in the Turkish-ruled Middle East, in the wake of Napoleon's military adventures in the region, gave rise to several curious plans to change that situation by introducing new railway lines on both sides of the Jordan River. As early as 1838, Sir Moses Montefiore (who visited Jerusalem in 1827, 1838, 1849, 1855, 1857, 1866, and 1875) envisioned a railway line between Jaffa and Jerusalem. He discussed the idea with Lord Palmerston, the British prime minister, and a meeting was organized with the Turkish Grand Vizier, Ali Pasha, during the latter's visit to London in May 1856. The inspired Vizier was persuaded to sign a British-Turkish agreement but in December, a message arrived from Istanbul that the Ottoman government was not willing to provide any land for the construction of the proposed line.

A second and similarly failed British plan, issued in 1856, recommended a short line from Jaffa to Lydda and a paved road for the remainder of the way to Jerusalem. In 1864, the German-American engineer, Charles Frederick Zimpel, approached the Ottoman authorities with a plan to build several railways in the Middle East. He spent a year in Constantinople, repeatedly and unsuccessfully trying to gain a concession for the new line, until that plan was abandoned, too.

Next in line was the German architect, Conrad Schick of Jerusalem, who published a detailed study of his own proposal for a railway to Jerusalem through the northern Judea Mountains. Other grand plans included a line to Jerusalem from Gaza and northern Sinai, in part along the same route of the later British-built standard gauge line of World War I.

Britain's interest in the Jerusalem railway project did not go unnoticed, attracting the attention of France and Austro-Hungary who had each their own political reasons for concerning themselves with the Turkish Empire, in this case through the construction of a railway line in the Holy Land. In the end, Turkish fears of Christian missionary activities, real or imagined, and the lack of sufficient funds to finance any of these plans, resulted in the complete absence of any railways in the Holy Land at a time when Europe and her colonies were busy building new lines everywhere. All, however, was not lost. Enter the Jerusalem entrepreneur, Yosef Navon.

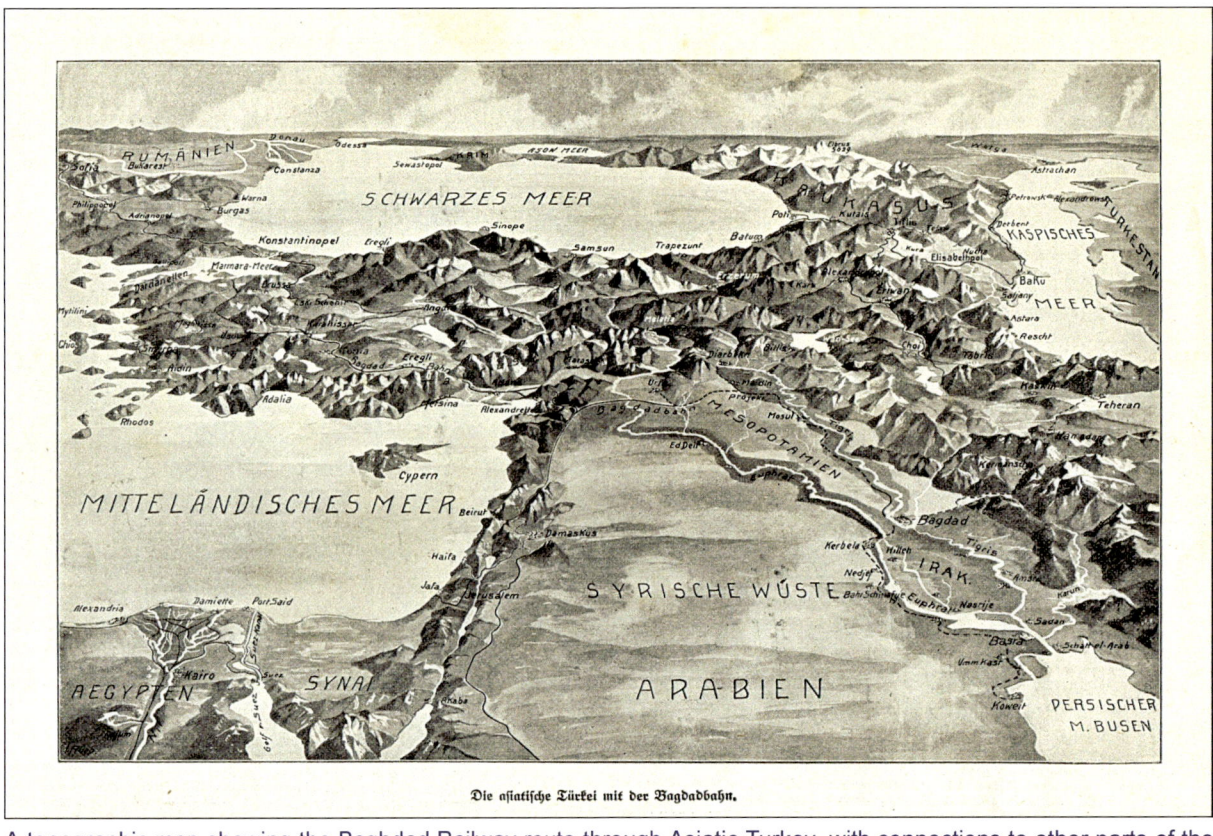

A topographic map showing the Baghdad Railway route through Asiatic Turkey, with connections to other parts of the Middle East and Africa.

Charles Zimpel's proposed railway plan of 1864.

National Library of Israel

JAFFA & JERUSALEM RAILWAY

The official inauguration ceremony of the new railway service between Jaffa and Jerusalem, on Sept 26, 1892. The station building is decorated with many Turkish Ottoman flags, and a Baldwin 2-6-0 steam locomotive is visible to the left, barely seen through the flags on its entire front end. A total travel time of four hours was needed to cover the distance between the two cities.

The Jaffa & Jerusalem Railway (J & J in short) was the first railway line in the Holy Land. It was built by the French company Société du Chemin de Fer Ottoman de Jaffa à Jérusalem et Prolongements and inaugurated in 1892, originally to the gauge of one metre. In World War I, the line was widened to the Hedjaz Railway gauge of 1,050 mm and following the British military advance and takeover of Jerusalem in the same war, to standard gauge.

The story of the J & J begins with Yosef Navon, a Jewish businessman from Jerusalem. As early as 1885, Navon became increasingly interested in the project, and in due time set out to promote his plan with the Turkish authorities in Constantinople. Being an Ottoman citizen, Navon's plan was viewed favourably and after three years of relentless persuasion, on 28th October 1888 he received the Sultan's concession for 71 years to build his line, with permission to extend it to Gaza and Nablus and without any financial guarantees from the Turkish Government. He then travelled to Europe, and in 1889 sold the concession to Bernard Camille Collas, a French lighthouse inspector, for one million francs. On 29 December 1889, the Jaffa & Jerusalem Railway Company was established in Paris. The company raised a capital of 14 million francs, mostly from Christian religious investors, and the actual construction work could now commence under European engineers with a native workforce. The groundbreaking ceremony was held on 31 March 1890 near Yazur (today a few miles to the east of Tel Aviv) with the attendance of the Turkish Governor of Palestine, Navon himself, and local dignitaries.

The first trial run was carried out in October 1890, with thousands of curious local spectators who had never seen a locomotive before. The first section, from Jaffa to Ramleh, was opened on 24 May 1891, with Dir Aban (دير آبان, 21 km to the west of Jerusalem) reached on 4th December. Both stations in Jaffa and Jerusalem were built outside the city limits under orders from the Turks, and in Jerusalem on land that was purchased from the Church at a record-setting price for any plot of land in and around the city walls.

History was made on 21st August, when the first train entered the city of Jerusalem. A week later, on 27th, the first Jerusalem-bound passenger train arrived from Jaffa behind a decorated Baldwin 2-6-0 locomotive and rolling stock imported from France. The line was officially inaugurated on 26th September 1892, and up to six hours were required to complete the journey, twice the somewhat optimistic planned travel time of only three hours in each direction. A grand event was held outside Jerusalem's new station building, and Yosef Navon, who had already been awarded the French Legion of Honour, received an Ottoman medal for his initiative and the honorary Turkish title of Bey.

The railway's financial problems began almost immediately upon the start of regular service, culminating in a deficit in the first year of operation. Tourist traffic was lower than expected, with only one daily train to Jerusalem and back and with an average speed that was slow enough that passengers could jump on and off the train with the least effort. The situation was improved in 1894, following a reorganization plan that appealed to new investors and thanks to a rise in the number of passengers and the volume of freight carried. The line is said to have become profitable in 1897, although a year later, in 1898, it was found to be bankrupt yet again despite the creation of several Jewish settlements along the railway's route.

The J & J survived the financial hardships and in 1904 the company decided to stock up with new Mallet steam locomotives from August Borsig of Berlin. The first of these arrived in 1905, and two more were added in 1908. A fourth Borsig locomotive was reportedly captured en route to Jaffa during World War I and sent to Alexandria, in several large boxes, and was never heard of again.

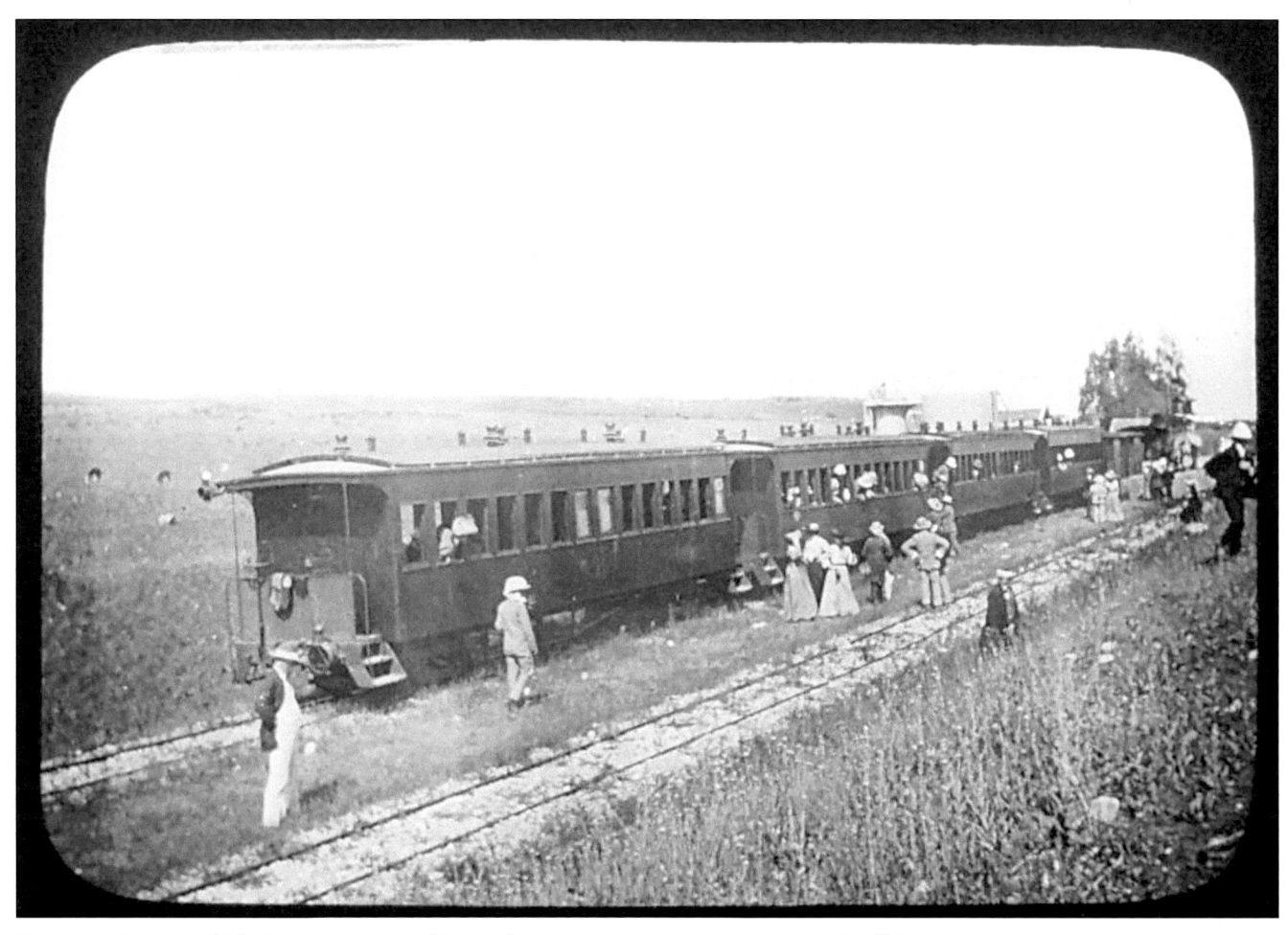

A panoramic view of Wadi Surar station with a Jaffa and Jerusalem passenger train in 1904.

A splendid view of Jerusalem train station in 1895, three years after officially inaugurating the service between Jaffa and Jerusalem. The locomotive is Baldwin 2-6-0 No. 4 "Lydda".

No. 60. Jerusalem Station (Palestine)

Official portrait of a new steam locomotive for the original Jaffa & Jerusalem Railway – Borsig 5464, built 1904, 0-4-4-0 No. 6 "Bittir". A total of four such locomotives were ordered for use on this line, of which three were delivered and the fourth was lost in WWI.

No. 6 "Bittir" is seen again in a rare photo taken between 1904 and 1917 near Ramleh. This was one of the first German locomotives in the Holy Land.

A rare picture of one of the Jaffa & Jerusalem Railway's five original Baldwin 2-6-0 steam locomotives at the head of a passenger train, possibly in Ramleh station in 1897.

A pre-WWI postcard showing a group of American sailors riding a train on the original (metre gauge) Jaffa to Jerusalem line. At the head of the train is one of the five American-built Baldwin 2-6-0 steam locomotives that were used on this route between 1892 and WWI. The locomotive appears to be taking water, somewhere in the Judean hills.

A pre-WWI view of a Jaffa & Jerusalem Railway mixed train, with Baldwin 2-6-0 steam locomotive No. 3 taking water at Sujud (or "Sejed") train station.
Israel Railways Museum

The first of five metre gauge 2-6-0 Baldwin steam locomotives, No. 1 "Jaffa", delivered to the Jaffa & Jerusalem Railway, as seen in Jerusalem station in 1904.

A rare glass slide showing Jerusalem station with a Jaffa & Jerusalem mixed train, prior to departure to Jaffa in 1910. At the head of the train is one of the line's three Borsig 0-4-4-0 steam locomotives. Partly visible in the background is the Montefiore windmill and Jerusalem's new city.

The train between Jaffa – Jerusalem.

A fantastic pre-WWI view of a complete Jaffa & Jerusalem mixed traffic train, with four passenger coaches, five freight cars, and one of the railway's three Borsig 0-4-4-0 steam locomotives.

A rare and unusual picture, probably taken in 1892 either in Jaffa or Jerusalem, of Baldwin 2-6-0 steam locomotive No. 1 "Jaffa". The locomotive is decorated with two Turkish flags, one flag on each side of the huge headlight, and a small crowd of exotically-dressed colonial and native spectators appears to have gathered for the special event. Strangely, the rails do not seem to be fixed to the wooden sleepers at all. Note the small pile of nails at the bottom left, the pickaxe in the middle, and the various tools on both sides of the track.

The rear of a passenger train, in a pre-WWI glass slide, probably at Sejed station (سجد). Regular refuelling stops were required to replenish the line's modest fleet of five (out of a total of eight, including three German-built Borsig Mallets) Baldwin 2-6-0 steam locomotives with a fresh supply of water, especially on the steep climb up the Judean hills to Jerusalem.

A passenger train is standing outside Dir A-Ban station, at the foot of the Judean hills, in this panoramic and pre-WWI photo. One of the five Baldwin 2-6-0s that operated on this line between 1892 and WWI is visible beyond the leading baggage van.

A strikingly clear picture of the short extension built into the Mediterranean Sea, within the Port of Jaffa. The extension was used to access the nearby station directly from the sea.

A pre-WWI view of Jerusalem station, showing the new station building and a train parked alongside the main platform. One of the railway's five 2-6-0s, built by Baldwin of Philadelphia in 1890/2, is visible beyond the station. Admiring the building's elegant architecture is a small group of youngsters.

The Société du Chemin de Fer Ottoman de Jaffa à Jérusalem et Prolongements issued this 500 Francs bond in 1894.

1890-built Baldwin 2-6-0 No. 3 "Ramleh" on the turntable at Jerusalem.

Library of Congress LC-M361-316

WORLD WAR I

A panoramic view of Jaffa station, close to the modern-day city of Tel Aviv, dated 19 November 1917. A passenger train, formed of three bogie coaches and one baggage van, is parked next to the main platform. Absent from the photo are the railway's Baldwin and Borsig steam locomotives, which were sabotaged and destroyed in the wake of the Turkish retreat and the successful British military advance from Egypt to the north in WWI.

On 28th June 1914, the Austro-Hungarian Archduke, Franz Ferdinand, was assassinated during an official visit to the city of Sarajevo. His death led to a political crisis which spread from the Balkans to all of Europe, whose major powers were divided into the Triple Entente (France, Russia and Britain) and the Triple Alliance (Germany, Austria-Hungary and Italy). A state of war existed between Germany and Russia as of 1st August 1914, signaling the start of the First World War and, after four years of unprecedented bloodshed in which millions were killed, the fall of the German, Austro-Hungarian and Turkish-Ottoman Empires.

Britain's intentions for the Turkish Empire were clear enough. The Turkish Sultan, who joined the war on the German Kaiser's side, was secretly called "the sick man on the Bosphorus" and with the war's outbreak, the moment had finally arrived to do away with the Turkish stranglehold in the Middle East for once and for all. This was achieved over the course of the war, albeit with strong Turkish opposition and a heavy loss of life on both sides.

The Turkish war effort relied on the railways to transport men and equipment to the front, in Turkish Palestine as in Mesopotamia. The J & J was taken over by the Turkish and German armies and Jaffa station became their military headquarters. In early 1915, the railway's machinery was sent uphill to Jerusalem, safely away from a possible British bombardment. Later in the same year, the western section of the line from Jaffa was dismantled as far as Lydda and the track was reused in the construction of the Hedjaz Railway to Beersheba. The remaining section, from Lydda to Jerusalem, was rebuilt to the Hedjaz gauge of 1,050 mm, connecting Jerusalem with the rest of the Turkish system.

The British advanced northwards from Egypt and in November 1917, facing defeat, the retreating Turks sabotaged the railway and damaged the locomotives, carrying away with them anything they could. The triumphant British Army repaired the line and Navon's railway was brought back to life. The first British train reached Jerusalem on 27th December 1917. Of the locomotives, five survived the war (Baldwin-built No. 3 and No. 5 and three of the Borsig 0-4-4-0s (Nos. 6, 7 and 8). All were scrapped, except for one pair of driving wheels from one of the Baldwin locomotives which is on permanent display at the Israel Railways Museum in Haifa.

THE HEDJAZ RAILWAY

Damascus Kanawat train station - 2-8-2 No. 254 (Hartmann 4023-34 / 1918) and passenger train. Photo taken between 1920 to 1946 (note the letter "H" (for "Hedjaz") on the freight car, to the left of the locomotive). A British officer, wearing a pith helmet, is keeping things in order.

The Hedjaz Railway ("Hicaz Demiryolu" in Turkish) was a giant Ottoman narrow gauge railway system that connected Damascus in Syria with Medina in Arabia, in total a distance of 1,300 km. "Hedjaz" (اَلْحِجَاز) means "barrier" in Arabic and refers to a region in western Arabia which is bordered by a mountain range separating it from the rest of the country. Later on, a branch line was built to Haifa and the Mediterranean Sea, and through the Samaria region southwards to Beersheba and Sinai. The railway was created with German support before World War I, officially to carry religious pilgrims to Medina and Mecca, the holy Muslim cities in Arabia. It only got as far as Medina and its main purpose, however, was to serve as a strategic Turkish line in the Middle East.

The story of the Hedjaz Railway has already been told elsewhere in great detail, covering the railway's history in Syria, Jordan and Arabia, that is, to the east of the Jordan River. For the purpose of this book, a review of the railway's western section (fondly known in Israel today as "The Valley Railway") is hereby given.

In addition to the Damascus-Medina main line, the Hedjaz Railway operated an extension from Deraa Junction, in southwestern Syria and thirteen km to the north of the border with Jordan, to Haifa. It was opened on 15th October 1905 and had eight stations, with a total distance of 95 km along the railway's route to Haifa from el Hamma, the first station after crossing the border from Syria. Another Hedjaz line proceeded due south from Afula Junction, off the Haifa branch, to Beersheba and onwards into Sinai, in preparation for a planned Turkish-German attack on the Suez Canal and Egypt. The western Hedjaz Railway remained active after the demise of the Turkish Empire, without the Beersheba extension but with regular passenger trains between Haifa and Damascus, until the final closure of the line in Israel in 1951. The Haifa-Bet Shean section, reopened on 16 October 2016, has been modernized and upgraded to standard gauge, with a new station in Bet Shean that cuts right through the few preserved remains of the old one.

The completion of the line to Haifa provided the Hedjaz Railway with an outlet to the Mediterranean Sea, through which construction materials, new locomotives and rolling stock could be received and agricultural goods dispatched to markets abroad.

Haifa station, inaugurated in 1908, was an eye-pleasing blend of German and Ottoman architecture. Right outside it, a tall monument was placed in honor of the Turkish Sultan, Abdul Hamid II. It was personally designed by the Sultan's chief palace architect, Raimondo Tommaso D'Aronco, and stands there to this day, a reminder of bygone times in Haifa's history. A local line to Akko was built in 1912. Freight and passenger traffic continued to grow steadily throughout the first few years of operation, and the travel time to Tiberias was cut down significantly thanks to a combined service, by train to Samach station and then by boat across the Sea of Galilee. The line achieved international recognition when, starting in 1906, it was included in the Thomas Cook travel agency's Holy Land tours, leading to the introduction of first class coaches in

2-8-0 No. 164 (Borsig Locomotive Works, Berlin 9013 / 1914) and passenger train in Naharayim (Jordan Valley) in the 1930s.
Library of Congress LC-M33- 3236

1912.

A British blockade in World War I caused a shortage of much-needed coal for the steam locomotives. This was partly solved by building several short branch lines into the forests around Mount Carmel, with natural wood now used instead of coal. Over time, these activities led to the systematic destruction of most of the coastline forests south of Haifa in the name of the Turkish war effort. It did the Turks no good and in the spring of 1918, British expeditionary forces were advancing to Syria, capturing the Haifa line in the process. Samach station was taken over, in a room to room battle, on 25th September 1918. Damascus was liberated from Ottoman rule on the first day of October. As was the case in Jerusalem, the retreating Turks destroyed and sabotaged as much of the railway's equipment as possible to prevent it from falling into enemy hands.

Mention should also be made of the Samaria line, which was supposed to connect Haifa with Jerusalem. The first seventeen km of track were constructed early on in 1913, descending from Afula Junction to Jenin and Messoudieh and splitting into two equally picturesque extensions, one to Nablus and another to Tul Karm. Political pressure from France may have played a role in the fact that the line was never completed as far as Jerusalem and instead, the Tul Karm branch was extended to Lydda, Beersheba and Sinai in World War I. The Samaria lines survived the war, with minimum traffic, and were ironically reactivated in 1940, during the British military operations in Syria. They have since then been abandoned and dismantled, sadly including Messoudieh station which was taken over by Israel in 1967 and demolished in 1975 in the wake of a failed attempt to establish an Israeli settlement there.

In the final years of the British Mandate in Palestine, mounting Jewish resistance to Britain's position on the question of an independent Jewish state took its toll on the railways. Attacks on trains and railway lines occurred regularly and on 16 June 1946, in a coordinated assault on rail and road bridges, the Hedjaz Railway bridge over the Yarmuk River was blown up shortly before midnight, at once cutting off the Haifa line from the rest of the Hedjaz system. Tragedy struck when on 20 September 1946, Haifa's beautiful Turkish train station was destroyed in another attack, along with the station's iconic clock tower and passenger waiting hall. The station was not rebuilt and a gap in the middle of the building marks the location of the ruined main part. Bruised and battered, the western Hedjaz Railway was practically put out of service, although a few trains continued to run from Haifa and as far as Afula after 1948. The line was eventually closed down in the early fifties and the rolling stock was either sold off or scrapped, except for Krauss-built steam locomotive No. 10 which has miraculously survived and is on static display inside the Israel Railways Museum's rolling stock shed, originally the Hedjaz Railway's locomotive depot in Haifa. An ambitious plan to restore a section of the original Hedjaz line in the Jordan Valley, using two new steam locomotives that are supposed to come from the Meiningen Locomotive Workshops in Germany, has been proposed but as of today still awaits approval.

The empty and abandoned loco shed at Samach station, to the south of the Sea of Galilee and Tiberias, in 1954. This beautiful shed was sadly demolished and completely removed from the site.

Israel Railways Museum

The bridge at Hamat Gader (el Hamma), as seen from the Israeli side of the border with Syria in November 2012.

A new Henschel 2-4-6-0 Mallet for the Hedjaz Railway.

Beersheba train station name is written in Arabic - Bir Saba. In this 2005 photo, the station building is in a generally poor condition. Things are different today, thanks to a massive renovation project.

0-6-0ST No. 32 "Jordan" (Hohenzollern Locomotive Works, Düsseldorf 1903 / 1905).

Haifa train station in 1919, with La Meuse 0-10-0T No. 2435 standing next to German-built 2-8-0T No. 71 (Jung 1212 / 1907). The picturesque town of Haifa is clearly visible beyond the station area.

Israel Railways Museum

2-6-0 No. 60 (originally No. 31) (Arnold Jung Locomotive Works 964 / 1906). This locomotive was abandoned in Medain Saleh.

2-8-0 No. 120 (originally No. 60) (Arnold Jung Locomotives Works 1201 / 1907).

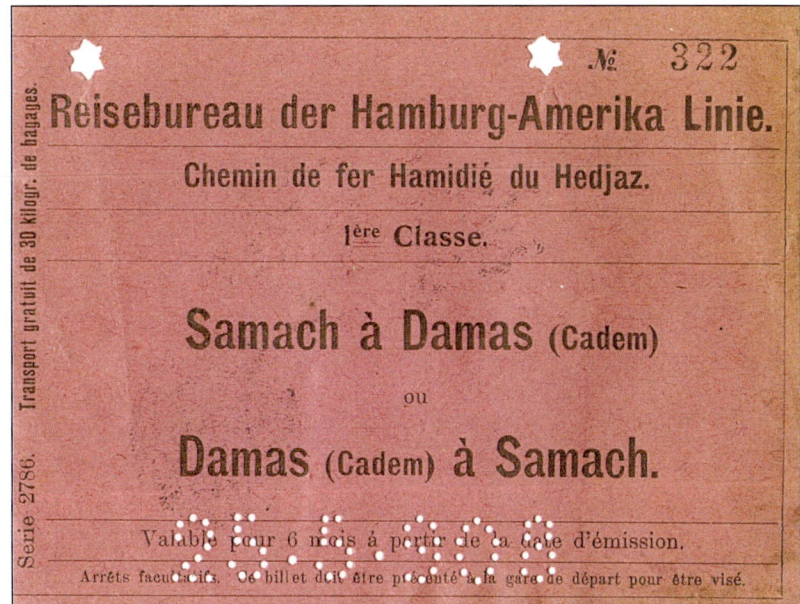

A Hedjaz Railway first class Samach-Damascus return ticket, issued by the Reisebureau der Hamburg-Amerika Linie on May 25, 1908.

An official photo of Turkish imperial officials posing in front of the new Hedjaz Railway monument in Haifa station, in 1905. Two new Krauss steam locomotives are seen in the background. Sadly, Haifa station was partly destroyed in a terror attack in September 1946, and has never been rebuilt since then.

Remains of the line in northern Samaria, as seen in the winter of 1995.

A panoramic view of Tel Yossef, with a train travelling in the distance, in 1949.

One of the last known photos of the station in Afula, probably in 1955. Amazingly, the track is still intact and several boxcars are clearly visible near the station building. The houses of a new neighbourhood are also seen beyond the station area. The whole line was dismantled shortly after this photo was taken.

The impressive Ottoman monument, erected in honour of the Hedjaz Railway and the Turkish Sultan, with the new locomotive workshops in the background. The entire pictured area has changed dramatically since this undated photo was taken, probably around 1910. The sea was pushed backwards as part of a major port development project. The handsome house to the left of the monument was demolished, as were sadly also the beautiful workshops, and the railway line was regauged following the British military advance from Egypt and eventual takeover of the Holy Land, in WWI. The Turkish monument was spared, thankfully.

Haifa railway station, possibly taken towards the end of WWI, showing the still complete station building and the amazingly empty Mount Carmel rising over the station area. A few freight cars are parked in the yard, and what appears to be a steam loco is partly visible right in front of the passenger hall.

A full pre-WWI view of the station in Haifa, showing the impressive station building with its clock tower.

26

A dramatic 1908 view of 0-6-0T No. 27 hauling a freight train across a new bridge over the Yarmuk Creek, on the main line from Haifa to Deraa Junction, in Syria. Extra water tanks were routinely needed for the journey in this dry area.

J.H. Halladjian

0-6-0T No. 11. Twelve such locomotives were built by Krauss of Munich between 1902 and 1905. Sister locomotive, No. 10, is on static display at the Israel Railways Museum in Haifa.

LOKOMOTIVFABRIK KRAUSS & COMP. AKTIENGESELLSCHAFT, München.

Ph. 566 b

Zylinder-Dchm.	540 mm	Heizfläche	65,94 qm	Kohlenraum	1100 kg		
Kolbenhub	500 "	Rostfläche	1,21 "	Wasserraum	3500 l		
Triebrad-Dchm.	930 "	Dampfüberdruck	12 Atm.	Zugkraft bei 50%	3730 kg		
Achsenstand	2500 "	Gewicht im Dienst	30,40 t	Spurweite	1050 mm.		

27

The morning sun shines brightly in this 1914 view of the Hedjaz Railway train station in Haifa, with Mount Carmel rising over the station area in the background. Following the successful British military campaign and the eventual takeover of the Holy Land in WWI, Haifa station became the starting point for international passenger trains to Cairo, Damascus and, in WWII, also to Beirut and western Lebanon. The handsome station building was partly destroyed in a terror attack in 1946, losing its elegant clock tower and entire main hall. Still a popular landmark in downtown Haifa, the station now serves as home for the Israel Railways Museum's archive as well as the historical rolling stock collection, in the former Hedjaz locomotive shed.

Panoramic view of the main line in the Yarmuk River Gorge, near El Hamma, to the east of the Sea of Galilee, leading from Haifa to Deraa Junction. Towering over the river and the rugged terrain is the railway bridge and the line is clearly marked along the hillside to the left.

Locomotive-tender à vapeur surchauffée pour voie de 1,050 mètre fournie au Syndicat du Chemin de Fer en Turquie d'Asie.

Poids en service . . . . 53 t.	Empattement . . . . 4,700 m.
Diamètre des roues . . . . 1,000 m.	Effort au crochet . . . . 8.985 k.

One of six La Meuse 0-10-0T steam locomotives built in 1914 for a customer in Turkey. Three were taken over by Britain in WWI and ended up on the Hedjaz Railway's western section.

A beautiful view (probably in 1915) of Messoudieh train station, on the main line from Afula Junction to Jenin and onwards, into Samaria, finally reaching the city of Nablus in the east and Tul Karm in the west. A loco is seen right next to the station building, and rising behind is the Herodesberg - the Roman settlement of Sebastia.

PALESTINE RAILWAYS

Practically a whole Hedjaz Railway train is about to enter the British workshops in Kantara for a major overhaul, following the British takeover of Palestine in WWI.
Israel Railways Museum

Britain's determination to win the Middle East from the Turkish Empire in World War I was placed in the capable hands of the Egyptian Expeditionary Force, resulting in an invasion of the Turkish-ruled territories on both sides of the Jordan River. By 1917, after a series of heavy battles, the Turks were on the run out of Beersheba and Jerusalem to Damascus and Aleppo. Suffering defeat, Turkey signed an armistice on 30 October 1918, ending four centuries of Ottoman Turkish imperial rule in western Asia. Syria and Lebanon were placed under French colonial administration. After a transition period under the Occupied Enemy Territory Administration (OETA), the British Mandate of Palestine, including the protectorate (later on, Emirate and Kingdom) of Trans Jordan, was created to administer the formerly Turkish territories.

In parallel to the British advance from Egypt, the standard gauge Sinai Military Railway (SMR) was built from Kantara, on the Suez Canal, across Sinai to El Arish, reaching Rafah in March 1917. The SMR relied on a curious fleet of British, American and even German locomotives, either on loan from the Egyptian State Railways or the spoils of war. These included antique locomotives built by Robert Stephenson in 1868, and 2-6-0s and 4-4-0s from Baldwin of Philadelphia. One German 0-6-0WT (Hanomag, 1913) was captured by the British Navy aboard a merchant ship in 1914, and ended up in Sinai.

Having reached Gaza in November 1917, the British standard gauge line was extended to Lydda Junction and Jerusalem. A new route, partly along the coastline, was built to Haifa which was reached from the south in late 1918. The actual working of both standard and narrow gauge trains was at first handed over to the newly-formed Palestine Military Railway (PMR) and, in October 1920, to the Palestine Railways (PR), a company officially owned by the Government of the British Mandate in Palestine. In between, in 1918 the PMR ordered 4-6-0 locomotives from Baldwin, the first ten of which arrived in Palestine in April 1919. The PMR also received a large shipment of 42 requisitioned London and North Western Railway 0-6-0s and 36 ex-London and South Western Railway 0395 Class 0-6-0s, all of them elderly machines that were phased out and scrapped with the arrival of new locomotives, although some of the LSWR units were kept for minor switching duties until 1936.

With the cessation of all hostilities in the Middle East, from 1920 PR introduced a daily mixed traffic train on the Haifa–Kantara line. An improvement in the hitherto uninspiring service standards was noted with the addition of Wagons Lits dining and sleeping cars three days a week until 1923, when the service was increased to daily. British Palestine received a new deep-water port in Haifa in October 1933, serving passenger and cargo ships in connection with the railways and replacing the Egyptian Port of Port Said, which until then served Palestine using a ferry across the Suez Canal at Kantara. Despite these efforts, passenger numbers dropped consistently due to growing competition with the public bus system to the point that in 1934, PR was left to carry little more than third class passengers. First class seats were routinely reserved for British government officials, high ranking officers and the occasional well-to-do traveller.

The period of quiet in Palestine came to an end in a series of wild disturbances and anti-Zionistic protests between 1936 and 1939 in the so-called Arab Revolt. The railways were perceived as a manifestation of the British policy in the country, and were accordingly subjected to regular sabotage and damage. Regular military patrols were arranged to keep the trains running, including the use of armored trucks which were converted for use on the railway. A British soldier was killed when his truck ran over a mine, and the patrol trucks were fitted with a small leading car in which Arab hostages were made to sit during the journey, in case another trackside mine was planted under the rails. Still, the attacks on the railways continued. In 1938 alone, 44 trains and 33 armoured trucks were derailed, 27 stations and 21 bridges were destroyed, and signalling and communication equipment was vandalised. Train movement after dark was suspended owing to the risk of sabotage. The combined result was a sharp drop in the demand for passenger trains, and a crisis from which PR never fully recovered.

A fantastic panoramic photo of the Port of Haifa and Haifa-East train station, with the impressive passenger hall still intact (note the Turkish-style clock tower). A variety of coaches, but strangely no locomotives visible, is occupying the switching yard and immediately beyond it are the Hedjaz Railway workshops, the turntable (to the right) and a Hedjaz administrative building (to the left). This same building, with the workshops, today houses the Israel Railways Museum. The entire area has changed dramatically since this photo was taken, some eighty years ago. The small houses were completely cleared away, and a modern seaport, stretching all the way to the warehouses at the top of the picture, was built over the same land.

Junction Station, Palestine. c1917. The station was where the Turkish railways to Beersheba and Gaza branch off from the Damascus to Jerusalem main line. A captured Turkish train is under the new command of the British Army.

An Australian troop train is under the command of Hedjaz Railway No. 2432, one of three 0-10-0T steam locomotives built by La Meuse in 1914. Photo possibly taken at Jenin (جنين) station, in the Samaria region, in the summer of 1941. This section of the line, leading from Afula Junction to Nablus and Tul Karm, was active in WWII, but was completely dismantled after the war. In November 1940, Australian Royal Engineers in Palestine began reconditioning the HR Railway from Tul Karm to Afula Junction. A New Zealand RE company ran three trains daily each way on that line from 6th June to 13th October, in connection with the military operations in Syria. The line was then closed until October 1944, when PR (which was in charge of the line) began operating freight trains in Samaria. The cost of reconditioning the line was met by the War Department.

Panoramic view of Haifa Bay and a part of the Hedjaz Railway switching yard, in a photo taken in the early 1920s, shortly after the successful British takeover of Palestine from Ottoman Turkey in WWI. Visible in the background are palm trees, along the Mediterranean Sea coastline, looking to the north. The top of a Hedjaz Railway 0-6-0ST steam locomotive, built by Krauss of Linz, is seen behind the passenger carriages, and additional steam locomotives are parked more to the left. Soon after this photo was taken, a new and modern port was built in Haifa, dramatically changing the small town's landscape. The palm trees, the sandy beach and the graceful coastline were all lost to progress, never to return.

32

Panoramic view of Haifa Bay and the western Galilee in the 1930s, showing the Hedjaz Railway train station to the right of the new Port of Haifa.

British officers are considering several ways to extract a La Meuse 2-6-2T steam locomotive, No. 2420, from the turntable pit in Jerusalem in 1918. Note the station building in the background.

Israel Railways Museum

Arab terrorists tore up several hundred yards of track on the railway line near Lydda in 1936, causing a train to be returned and checked. A collective fine of £5,000 was imposed on the population of Lydda and when payment was not forthcoming, tanks and armoured cars were sent to enforce payment. The photo shows British troops changing from one train to another after the Arabs had made one line impassable.

PR 4-6-4T steam locomotive No. 14 (Baldwin).

Israel Railways Museum

ONE OF FIVE 4—6—0 BALDWIN TENDER LOCOMOTIVES ACQUIRED BY THE WAR DEPARTMENT IN 1918, CONVERTED TO 4—6—4 TANK LOCOMOTIVES, 1937–38.

Official portrait of Clayton-built Palestine Railways third class passenger coach No. 329. PR owned six of these 120 seaters (Nos. 329-334).

Israel Railways Museum

The southbound passenger train from Haifa to Egypt is ready to pull out of Haifa Central station, on the long journey across the Sinai Desert and the Suez Canal to Cairo. Photo taken in the 1930s.

Israel Railways Museum

TRAIN LEAVING HAIFA STATION FOR EL KANTARA (SUEZ CANAL).

The most iconic Palestine Railways photo, with the beautiful Haifa East station building still intact in the background and a splendid view of the Cairo Express train (note Wagons Lits coaches) about to depart on the long journey across the Sinai Desert to Africa. Baldwin 4-6-0 steam locomotive No. 892 is in charge of this prestigious service.

Israel Railways Museum

Official portrait of Palestine Railways first class coach No. 120. Ten of these coaches (45 seats) were built by the Birmingham Railway & Carriage Works (PR Nos. 120-129).

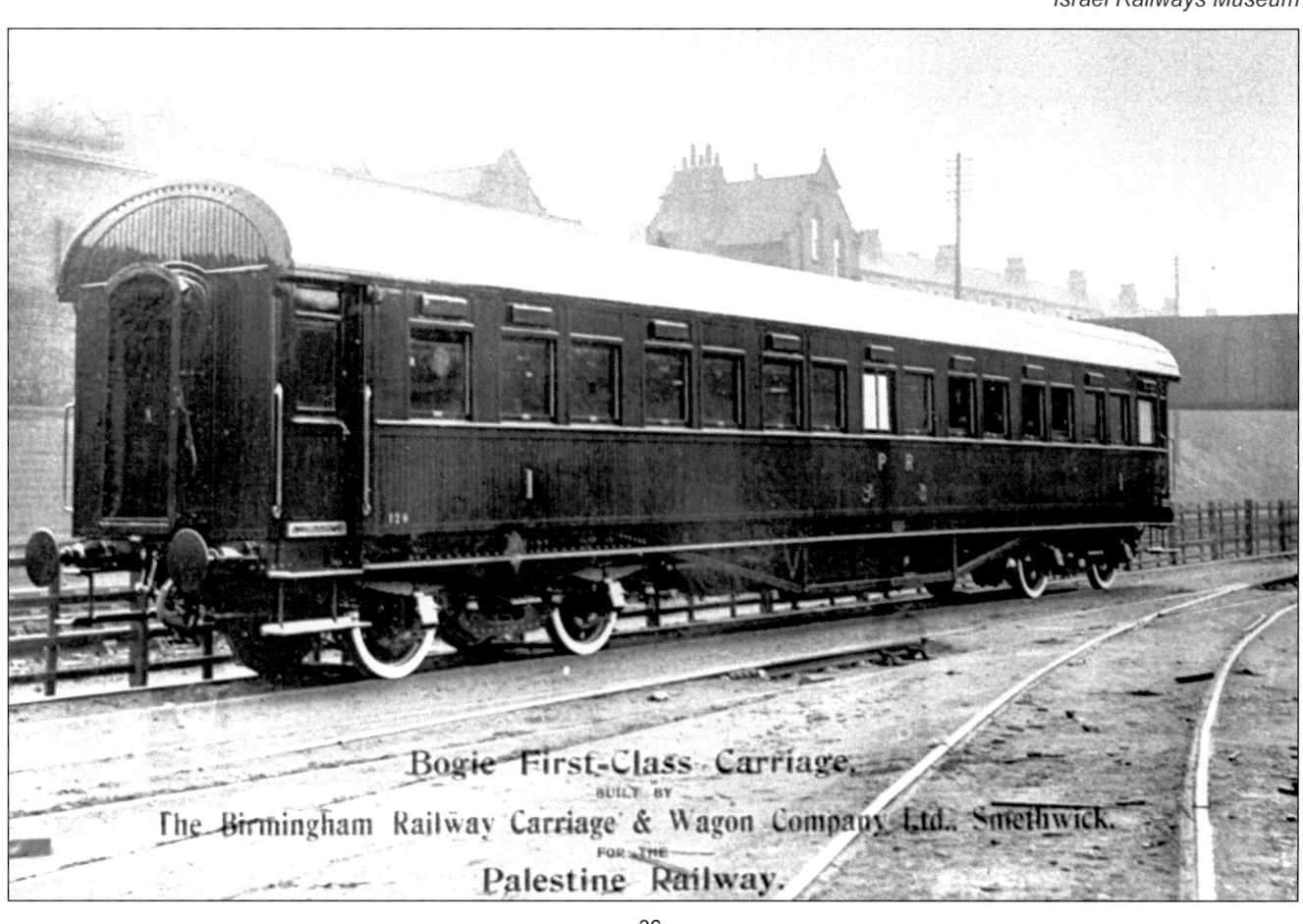

Israel Railways Museum

Bogie First-Class Carriage,
BUILT BY
The Birmingham Railway Carriage & Wagon Company Ltd. Smethwick.
FOR THE
Palestine Railway.

The unfortunate result of a turntable accident / deliberate sabotage in Jerusalem, with a derailed Hedjaz Railway locomotive and a small group of spectators nearby. Exact date in WWI unknown.

This undated photo shows the remains of a sabotaged Baldwin steam locomotive in Jerusalem.

Class K 2-8-4T heavy freight locomotive No. 1. For the steep gradients from Jaffa to Jerusalem, in 1922 PR obtained six new engines from Kitson in Leeds, specifically designed to be powerful enough for the Jerusalem service. They had 1,220 mm driving wheels, a diameter suitable for low-speed freight work and also for mountain gradients. The track gauge on the tight curves on the Jerusalem branch was widened from 1,435 mm to as much as 1,467 mm, but unfortunately even with this adjustment the heavy eight-coupled class K was unsuitable and suffered a number of derailments.

The enormous damage caused to the Cairo-Haifa express train and the main line is clearly evident in this 1940s photo of the aftermath of a terror attack on a train near Rehovot, 29th February 1948.

The wreckage of a freight train, derailed by explosives placed on the track, is strewn along an embankment five kilometres away from Jerusalem, 19th March 1947. The driver was killed in the attack and the fireman was injured. Locomotive No. 10 was damaged severely when it left the rails and fell over.

A colourised post-WWI glass slide of Jerusalem railway station.

A Palestine Railways passenger train, probably on the long-haul route to Egypt, with Baldwin No. 892 in an undated photo. Note the leading CIWLT coach.

Two Arab hostages are occupying the front-most seats of a Royal Engineers Regiment mine-sweeping trolley, in an attempt to stop the countless attacks on Palestine's railway system in 1938.

North British built 4-6-0 No. 61 at Lydda Junction in 1936.

The derailed and heavily damaged Haifa-Kantara express train, following a terror attack on the Palestine Railways in 1938. Note the Wagon Lits coach to the right.

Israel Railways Museum

Two views of the aftermath of different terror attacks in 1938.

British soldiers about to depart from Tel Aviv to Egypt in 1939.

The Turkish-built station in Haifa in the 1930s, showing passengers getting off a boat and ready to board a Palestine Railways train, within the station area. Rising over the station building is Mount Carmel. The large Hedjaz Railway building, to the left, now serves a new role as the main archive of the Israel Railways Museum.

P class 4-6-0 steam locomotive No. 65 at Lydda Junction on 25th January 1945. Six of these mixed traffic locomotives were built by the North British Locomotive Works in 1935 (NBL 24219-24).

A fascinating WWI photo of the first British standard gauge ambulance train on the originally narrow gauge railway line from Jaffa to Jerusalem, somewhere in the Judean hills outside the city. An ex-LSWR Adams 0-6-0 locomotive is in charge of this train.

Israel Railways Museum

A WWI photo of Jerusalem train station, shortly after the British takeover of the city from the Ottoman Army. Ex-LSWR 0-6-0 steam locomotive No. 28 (Neilson 3454/1885) (note former owner's initials on the tender) is facing a passenger train made of Egyptian coaches (partly clerestory), right outside the station building. Senior British officers were often in the habit of using such elegant coaches, and this could therefore be General Allenby's train to Jerusalem, following the upgrading of the track to standard gauge.

Israel Railways Museum

A rare photo of a British military train in Palestine, during WWI, on the main line from Egypt to Haifa. Trailing behind the Baldwin-built Egyptian State Railways 4-4-0 steam locomotive is a six-wheeled van, a complete London & South Western Railway (LSWR) ambulance train, and what appears to be several more baggage vans. Note the three men, perhaps also the driver and his fireman, in front of the train. Ten of these locos were supplied to the ESR, Nos. 602 - 611 (Baldwin Locomotive Works 18129 - 18131 and 18149 - 18155 / 1900).

A view of Jerusalem station in WWI, with ex-LSWR steam locomotive No. 28 (Neilson 3454 / 1885) at the head of a British military ambulance train.

P Class 4-6-0 steam locomotive No. 60 (North British, 24219/1935) stands ready to haul High Commissioner for Palestine, Lord Gort.

Panoramic view of downtown Haifa and the Mediterranean Sea, taken from Mount Carmel in the 1930s. Three Palestine Railways passenger coaches, and several boxcars, are parked close to the waterfront. A large warship, thought to be the Royal Navy's HMS Barham, is sailing out of the bay into the open sea. Note the Turkish clock tower, half-visible to the extreme left - a remnant of pre-WWI Ottoman rule in the Middle East.

Official delivery photo of Palestine Railways third class passenger coach No. 338, built by the Gloucester Railway Carriage & Wagon Company in 1935. It is here seen being lowered off the ship at the port of Haifa. A second new coach is visible on the platform, in the background. Standing right behind and overshadowing the Christen-Smith ship is the Italian luxury ocean liner, S. S. Roma, on a cruise in the Mediterranean Sea.

Haifa, new station in 1946.

Library of Congress 13535

An unidentified 4-6-0 on a branch of the Hedjaz to Hafir El Auja and El Qusaima via Beersheba in the Negev Desert.
Library of Congress 22026

This is thought to show the train at Haifa which brought Ethiopian Emperor Haile Selassie I and his family to Jerusalem, May 8, 1936.
Library of Congress 20219

WORLD WAR II AND THE HAIFA-BEIRUT-TRIPOLI RAILWAY

A panoramic view of the Lebanese coastline, with the road climbing up to the casino and the Haifa, Beirut & Tripoli Railway line curving gently around the edge of the cliff.

World War II broke out on 1st September 1939, with Nazi Germany's invasion of Poland and Britain's declaration of war on the Third Reich. Within a short time, the essentially European dispute assumed global proportions, sending shockwaves that were felt also in British Palestine. All at once confronted with a new challenge, Palestine Railways were expected to meet the many military demands of the British war effort both in the Middle East and in the deserts of North Africa. In 1940, the Haifa-Kantara railway became a vital supply route for the Allied forces in Egypt and Libya, right up to the German surrender in Tunisia in May 1943. Syria and Lebanon obeyed the orders from Vichy France, to the point that in June 1941, British forces rolled into these two countries, in part also to establish a new railhead on the Syrian coastline.

The standard gauge line from Egypt only got as far as Haifa, with a break in the route due to the ferry crossing of the Suez Canal. The line now had to be extended across the border with Lebanon and this duty was entrusted to South African Army engineers, who built the first section of what would eventually become the Haifa – Beirut – Tripoli (HBT) Railway. Skirting Haifa Bay to Akko, the HBT had to overcome a major natural obstacle in the form of the Rosh Hanikra limestone cliffs, using two railway tunnels at the foot of the cliff and retaining walls over the sea. The South Africans were transferred to other duties and the honour of completing the line was given to Australian and New Zealand Railway Groups, with the interesting outcome that in 1942, Haifa station was the starting point for destinations in three different continents – Cairo in Egypt, Damascus in Asia, and via Aleppo and Istanbul to mainland Europe.

Simultaneously with the HBT railway, in June 1941 Australian Engineers started building a new line alongside the Suez Canal southwards from Kantara, connecting with the Egyptian railway system in July over the El Ferdan swing bridge. Through Haifa-Cairo services commenced in August of the same year. The upgraded line allowed for uninterrupted travel by train from Egypt to Lebanon and the transfer of more than two million tons of freight in 1943-44, all this despite the heavy wear of the already overused trains, the wartime maintenance difficulties, and even a rainstorm and washout in November 1944 that derailed the Kantara-Haifa train, killing seven passengers and injuring forty.

PR alone could under no circumstances deal with the dramatic rise in traffic and it was therefore supplied with War Department 2-8-0s, the ROD type also known as the Great Central Railway Class 8K of 1911, and the more recent London, Midland and Scottish Railway Class 8F that was designed by William Stanier in 1935. Both types were sent to the Middle East and by June 1942, 24 ROD locomotives were running in Palestine and Lebanon. They were replaced in 1944 with LMS 8Fs from the Trans Iranian Railway. American USATC (S200) 2-8-2s arrived in the Middle East in 1942, 27 of which were also sent to Palestine and Lebanon and two S100 0-6-0Ts were given switching duties in Palestine. These locomotives were largely withdrawn before the end of the war in 1945, with 24 of the LMS 8Fs and the two S100s left behind in Palestine. American-built Whitcomb diesel-electric locomotives were sent to work on the HBT in the summer of 1943 and in December, more units were received in Palestine. None remained in the Middle East after the war and they were all sent to Italy.

Remains of the HBT line at Rosh Hanikra cliff in 1959. This potentially important route was proposed as a post-WWII rail link between Africa and Europe, but was eventually abandoned following the political problems in the Middle East and the closure of the Israeli-Lebanese border. Note the "beware - border!" board in Hebrew, at the entrance to the railway tunnel. The track (still perfectly intact in this picture) was gradually dismantled over the following years, with the last remains finally removed and the trackbed now used as a local road leading into the tunnel.

A view, taken in 1945, of the blockhouse at Jbeil, on the western Lebanese coastline, to the north of Beirut.

A 1940s photo of a War Department (ROD) 2-8-0 steam locomotive (ex-LNER Robinson Class O4) with a short train (four wheel auxiliary water tank and USATC brake van) at the portal of one of the HBT tunnels, near Rosh Hanikra (Ras Naqura).

A lighter carrying a locomotive approaches a wharf at a Syrian port during World War II.
Alexander Turnbull Library, Wellington, New Zealand

New Zealand Engineers unloading a locomotive from a ship at a Syrian port during World War II on 22 May 1942.
Alexander Turnbull Library, Wellington, New Zealand

A fascinating view of the Lebanese coastline near Beirut in 1982, with a group of Israeli tanks standing right next to the heavily damaged Haifa-Beirut railway line.

A passenger train is pulling into the first tunnel at Rosh Hanikra.

THE END OF THE BRITISH MANDATE IN PALESTINE

The final three years of Britain's rule in Palestine were a period of political and social chaos brought on by Jewish, Arab and even British terror attacks. Already in 1945, in the face of Britain's unrelenting refusal to let Jewish refugees and survivors of the Nazi persecution into Palestine, Zionist paramilitary organizations joined forces and openly declared war on the British administration and any British civilian and military assets that were present in the country, pending a change in the British policy on Jewish immigration to Palestine. Britain's primary concern at the time was the possible rise of communism in the Arab world, and political and financial interests dictated a policy that would keep the Arabs on the British side at all costs. Letting more Jews into British Palestine would have alienated the Arabs and the inevitable result was a civil war in Palestine, extremely damaging to the railway system. Locomotives, trains, stations, bridges and maintenance facilities were all blown up, sabotaged and ruined as a matter of routine. In 1946-7 alone, a pay train was robbed, the railway workshops in Haifa were partly destroyed, the western Hedjaz Railway was cut off from the Damascus-Amman main line, Haifa and Jerusalem stations were bombed, six policemen were killed when their trolley ran over a mine and the Cairo-Haifa express was derailed. The worst was yet to come. On 29 February 1948, 28 British soldiers were killed when their train was bombed near Rehovot, south of Tel Aviv. A month later, on 31 March, a mine exploded under a passenger train in Binyamina, south of Haifa, with forty casualties. Incredibly, in spite of the repeated attacks, the extensive damage to the railways and the loss of life, a plan was issued to link the railways of Africa, Asia and Europe through Palestine. It was a practical plan, given the direct line from Cairo to Haifa, Beirut and Aleppo, where passengers could connect with the Taurus Express to Istanbul and Europe, or in the opposite direction to Baghdad and the Persian Gulf. Regrettably, in 1946 the Lebanese government took over the HBT line, and traffic to Haifa was disrupted. The direct service to Egypt was similarly taken over by the Egyptian State Railways as far as Rafah, effectively cutting the line into two separate sections.

With the end of the British Mandate in Palestine already in sight, public security deteriorated even further. In a letter from 17 February 1948, addressed to the Chief Secretary of the Mandate Government, the last General Manager of Palestine Railways, Arthur F. Kirby, gave an honest and touching description of the services provided by the railways in British Palestine in spite of the challenging circumstances of a world war, crippling terror attacks on the system and the partly outdated equipment. In three pages, he tells the story of the Palestine Railways and his letter is repeated here, word for word, as the voice of reason and sanity in a country and a region where religion and politics are still allowed to go hand in hand to this day.

"In view of the imminent liquidation of the Palestine Railways Administration as it now exists, I feel that I should make some attempt to bring to the public some realisation, however small, of the services that the Palestine Railways have rendered to Palestine. Since I have been in Palestine, I have neither seen nor heard any real public appreciation of the railways, which have been taken for granted, or regarded as a concern upon which to pour contempt or to level abuse and virulent criticism. The railways have been also chosen as an easy target by political dissidents. During the many years of unrest in Palestine, bullets have been poured at railway staff honestly and conscientiously performing their duties as public servants, and bombs and mines have been used to wreck trains and destroy railway installations. Yet, neither the railway management nor its loyal staff have flinched from determination to keep railway services operating. I think it is important for the public of Palestine, whatever their race or creed, to realise the praiseworthy manner in which railway staff have taken trains out by day and by night in all weathers, fair and foul, in conditions which have been highly dangerous and usually with no personal defence against saboteurs, attacking and wrecking trains from hiding places, or large bands of robbers.

I wonder if the average person in Palestine realises the heartbreaking task of railway administration and operating officers in keeping things going against the heavy odds? It has not been by just waving a wand that bridges have been repaired and the line made fit for trains within a few hours of destruction, nor has it been by taking thought that locomotives wrecked by mines have been repaired time and time again so that most of them, though blown up several times, are still working after 28 years of service – and working efficiently.

I think it as well to mention these things because just recently I have heard so much derogatory talk about the railways and have been astonished to learn of the calumny which is being poured upon the railway management by people who should know better. I do not expect people outside the railway to appreciate fully the great technical difficulties which have had to be surmounted to keep the railways going, but I do expect that the public should show some appreciation of the altogether remarkable loyalty of the railway staff, both Arab and Jew, which has been so vital a factor in enabling the railways to continue to deliver goods. During the war, the Palestine Railways successfully coped with an increase in traffic unequalled, in relation to its normal volume, by any other railway. Since the war it has continued to operate under conditions comparable only with those which might exist in a country of war; yet, the railways keep operating with an efficiency which can be favourably compared with any neighbouring railways. Without the railways, Palestine would not have reached its present stage of industrial development.

To come to the present day, let me dispel some wrong impressions which have been fostered regarding the scale of thefts of goods in transit upon the Palestine Railways. It is probably not generally realised that thousands of tons of goods are moved daily by rail. The problem of the railway management is to continue to move those thousands of tons in a country where security is deteriorating. Every possible expedient is adopted to keep the traffic moving and the railway staff generally have pride in maintaining the service at all costs. The following circular was issued to the staff January last, in the confident knowledge that it would receive a loyal response:

KEEP THE RAILWAY GOING

The Palestine Railways have passed through difficult periods in the past years, but we have always managed to keep working. We are now passing through another difficult period and I know that all the railway staff will agree with me when I say that we shall try to keep working just the same as always. The railway is a commercial and non-political undertaking and our aim must be to maintain the railway services because they are essential to the community as a whole, no matter what race or creed.

The railway staff has worked together in amity and are known for their loyalty to duty. We have loyalty to our duty as railway men irrespective of our race or religion and we must take care to avoid any partisan spirit which might upset smooth working relationships between us as railway men performing our duties.

I wish to assure the staff that the management is fully conscious of the hazardous conditions of working and that I am endeavouring at all times to ensure the provision of as much security as I can obtain in present conditions, but we have to realise that we are working in a country which, unfortunately, is not at peace, and that we have to take risks in the performance of our duties and in obtaining our livelihood.

I know that I can confidently rely upon the loyalty and good sense of the staff to see us through and I exhort every member to do his utmost to persuade his friends, and the community generally, of the importance of ensuring that the railway staff are not interfered with in the course of performing their duties as public servants.

An indication of what is being made and of the loyalty of the staff is that even today, ten or more trains operate each way daily between Haifa and Lydda, carrying essential supplies, while the railway between Lydda and Jerusalem is fully occupied in the conveyance of essential supplies and exports. The export of this season's citrus crop is due in no small measure to the railways. This is not achieved without effort and suffering. We have no fewer than fifty personnel of the train crews absent from duty, some in hospital, suffering from the effect of having been interfered with while trying to perform their duties. Running trains are subject to attack and the principal marshalling depot is constantly being fired over by snipers. Only a loyal staff would continue working in such conditions.

The reports of losses from the railway have been exaggerated. These losses are serious in themselves, but they have been comparatively small compared with the total tonnage conveyed. Since train robberies first began in December last, less than seventy tons of wheat have been lost, about 120 tons of barley, 28 tons of rice and 200 tons of flour. Not more than forty tons of sugar in all has been lost. To any transport organisation, losses of goods on this scale while in their custody is heartbreaking, but it must be realised that the losses take place despite the efforts of the railway to achieve safe delivery. During the period, the railway conveyed no less than a total tonnage of about 200,000 tons. Of this over 30,000 tons was essential foodstuffs for civil consumption and the losses mentioned should be reckoned against these totals. The railway management takes the view that it is better to get through with 99% even at the risk of train robberies and other sabotage.

It is lamentable that dissident forces have been so persistent that after several weeks of ding-dong struggle in repairing the line between Lydda and Tel Aviv, and Jaffa, we have had to relinquish operation. Repair gangs working day and night and train crews being shot at can keep up no longer. The railway management would like nothing better but to be able to reopen this line. Similarly with the Petah Tiqva line which is being operated only under the greatest difficulties and with frequent interruption because of the destructive work of sabotage. It must be remembered that the railway administration, whether dealing with railways or ports, is a transport concern and has no security forces of its own.

My object in writing this letter to you is not only with the object of evoking some real appreciation of the work which the railway is performing and of the loyalty of its staff, but also to appeal to all parties concerned to endeavour to sink all political differences so far as the railway operation is concerned. In my opinion, the uninterrupted continuance of the railways and ports is vital to the stability of the country. Finally, let me emphasise that so long as the present railway management exists, it will endeavour to maintain the railways and ports as fully as possible without fear or favour and irrespective of politics."

Kirby's brave words fell on deaf ears. In the final days of the British Mandate in Palestine, during May 1948, railway services had effectively ceased. Kirby's own car was stolen at gunpoint. Fire erupted inside the railway's head office in Haifa, following an attack, with countless records and files tragically going up in smoke. Britain's undignified departure left the Palestinian Arabs dispossessed and the Jewish state fighting for its life. The smell of war was hanging in the air for years and for the remainder of 1948, passenger traffic was limited to the Haifa Bay area and the northern coastline.

ISRAEL RAILWAYS

In the morning hours of 14 May 1948, the last British High Commissioner in Palestine, Sir Alan Cunningham, boarded a ship out of Haifa, thereby ending thirty years of British rule in the Holy Land. That same day in Tel Aviv, at four in the afternoon, David Ben Gurion declared Israel as an independent Jewish state, only to watch the young Israel being cast into a war on all fronts with her neighbouring Arab countries. In the midst of fighting, the new Israel State Railways were created, replacing the Palestine Railways which ceased all operations upon the termination of the British Mandate. Similarly terminated were the international routes to Egypt, Lebanon and Syria, owing to the state of war with Israel, as well as the badly damaged western Hedjaz Railway. In central Israel, regular traffic on the Jerusalem line did not start until 1950, due to the precarious military situation to the west of Jerusalem. The Arab armies were defeated in the war, although east Jerusalem and the Samaria and Judea regions were under hostile Jordanian occupation, and railway services in Israel were slowly resumed.

ISR's first step was to secure the expert services of Alfred E. Perlman, President of the Penn Central Transportation Company and its predecessor, the New York Central Railroad. Perlman came to Israel in 1950 as a special consultant, expectedly recommending in his report that modernisation, namely dieselisation, should occur at the earliest possible opportunity for higher productivity and overall efficiency. However, before any of his suggestions could be implemented, it was first necessary to consider the military restrictions in the wake of the recent war.

Having successfully repelled the invading Arab armies, Israel gained control over the formerly Palestine Railways main line from Haifa to Ashkelon. The rest of the line, to Gaza and Kantara, was held by Egyptian forces which advanced into Israel from northern Sinai, coming within a distance of only thirty km from Tel Aviv before retreating back to Gaza. The Iraqi invasion was crushed in a decisive battle to the east of Bet Shean, after nearly reaching the coastline halfway between Haifa and Tel Aviv. The Jordanian Legion was pushed back into Samaria, leaving a section of the Haifa-Lydda line in Jordanian hands near the Arab city of Tul Karm. Armistice agreements were signed in 1949 with Egypt on 24th February, with Jordan on 3rd April, with Lebanon on 23rd March and with Syria as late as 29th July, due to another outbreak of widespread riots in that country, with the effect that the Haifa-Lydda line was formally included in the agreement with Jordan and passengers were amusingly warned "do not lean out of the country!" when passing through Tul Karm station. The Hedjaz line out of Haifa remained in Israel all the way to the border with Syria, but without the Nablus and Tul Karm branches in Samaria. The first Israeli train entered Jerusalem station on 7th August 1949. Regular service to Jerusalem began on 2nd March 1950.

A fleet of Palestine Railways, War Department (including two ex-Wehrmacht Regelspur diesels) and Hedjaz Railway steam locomotives was left behind in Israel in 1948. This was gradually phased out in the 1950s in favour of diesels, with the first three coming from Société Anglo-Franco-Belge in 1952. Two years later, in 1954, ISR began to stock up with General Motors (EMD) type G12 diesel locomotives and, as part of the 1952 Reparations Agreement between Israel and the Federal Republic of Germany, with three German-made diesel switchers built by Deutz and eighteen Maschinenfabrik Esslingen diesel locomotives. The age of steam in Israel was over by 1959. Thirteen more G12s arrived from EMD in the sixties. Curiously, four other G12s were captured from Egypt in 1967, together with three G16s, one G8 and rolling stock, a repeat of the 1956 war with Egypt in which five Borsig and North British 2-6-0s ended up in Israel, of which one was wrecked in the war and four were used in Israel.

Also in the 1950s, changes to the national railway system were carried out. A new coastal route was completed in 1954, directly linking Haifa with Tel Aviv and replacing the old PR main line which required a change of trains in Lydda Junction, and had been exposed to Jordanian fire and Arab hostilities ever since 1948. The new line to Beersheba, inaugurated in 1956, was gradually extended to Dimona and into the phosphate mines in the Negev Desert. In Tel Aviv, the line leading to Jaffa station was abandoned, and a new terminal was built in a remote location in the south of the city for southbound trains to Jerusalem and Beersheba.

A satisfied customer, in the 1970s ISR ordered nine powerful type G26CW diesels from EMD to haul heavy mineral trains from the phosphate mines in Oron to the port of Ashdod. Six more EMD diesels, type G26CW-2, and a single GT26CW-2, arrived in the 1980s for the coal traffic to the Ashkelon electric power station. One other diesel, a T44 built by Kalmar Verkstad of Sweden, was purchased in the late eighties.

Similarly inherited was an ageing fleet of Palestine Railways wooden passenger coaches, manufactured in Britain, mostly in the 1920s, and in a generally unsuitable condition. In 1955, eight 96-seat standard class steel coaches were ordered in Germany from Orenstein & Koppel and in 1961, fourteen more arrived from the Aubevoye (Normandy) based French manufacturer, Carel et Fouché. 43 coaches were built for service in Israel by Boris Kidrič of Yugoslavia starting in 1964. Bought second-hand from British Rail, in 1977 ISR introduced eight Mark IIc TSO (Tourist Standard Open) coaches (BR Nos. M5567, 5570, 5575, 5580, 5588, 5593, 5606 and 5612) that were supposed to set a higher travel standard on Israel Railways, but soon proved inadequate in the hot and humid Mediterranean climate. They were fitted with air conditioners in 1989 (except for M5580) and were gone by 1997. One coach, BR No. M5570, is on display at the railway museum in Haifa.

A peculiar episode in Israel's railway history took place in 1956, with the arrival of twelve three-car diesel-hydraulic trains from West Germany. These trains, built by Maschinenfabrik Esslingen in Mettingen, near Stuttgart, together with Linke Hofmann Busch (LHB) and Waggon und Maschinenbau Donauwörth (WMD), were paid for using German government funds from the above-mentioned Reparations Agreement and were based on the German Federal Railways (Deutsche Bundesbahn) VT 08 multiple units. Elegant and stylish, and easily recognized with their round, egg-like ends (hence the nickname "Eierkopf" or "egghead"), the trains were equipped with one 1,000 hp diesel motor powering a Maybach Mekydro transmission unit. 248 seats were available in total, of which forty were second class, in a power car, coach and trailer configuration. Later on, ten more intermediate coaches were added, giving a higher capacity of 348 seats in four cars. An unfortunate combination of technical problems, ranging from cracked wheels to seawater damage and gearbox failures, together with inappropriate maintenance and misuse, resulted in the rapid decline of the Esslingen trains. The diesel motors were eventually removed and the trains were converted to ordinary locomotive-hauled passenger stock until 1979. In 1992, seven of the intermediate coaches were literally brought back from the dead after twenty years and, having been thoroughly refurbished in the railway workshops, were put back in service for a couple more years. It has been suggested that ISR's refusal to buy new diesel trains in the following years was specifically because of the serious problems experienced with the Esslingen sets.

Be that as it may, starting in the 1970s, a period of stagnation and austerity appears to have set in and ISR entered an era of little development and growth. This was reflected in the number of passengers carried and the government's policy of placing a higher priority on building new roads and highways, rather than buying new trains and building new lines. The opening of the Tel Aviv-Jerusalem highway had a deadening effect on the Jerusalem line. In 1995, the service was reduced to only one train a day in each direction, the same as a century ago. On 12 July 1998, Israel Railways was left with no other choice but to temporarily close the line, with the last train running on 14 August 1998. A change of fortune, however, was coming.

ISR's luck was on the rise again in 1988, when it was merged with Israel's Ports Authority and money was available for modernisation. The passenger coaches were upgraded and fitted with roof mounted air conditioners. The single track Haifa-Tel Aviv main line was doubled and the Ayalon link in Tel Aviv was completed. New IC3 diesel trains were introduced in 1990, setting a new level of travel comfort, and more local and suburban trains were added to the timetable, with the happy result that from thirty passenger trains a day in 1989, by 2005 there were no fewer than 288 trains (local and long-haul) carrying over twenty million passengers per year, ten times more than in 1989. To meet the demand, ISR even bought in 1994 eight ex-SNCF Inox coaches (scrapped in 2006, one coach preserved). In 2003, ISR became a government owned company. The increase in traffic volume reached 150 freight trains and 525 passenger trains per day in 2016, serving more than 64 million passengers in 2017.

A large scale fleet renewal program was set in motion in the late nineties, with an initial batch of new Alstom diesel locomotives in 1998. In 2011, fourteen Euro 3200AC and fifteen Euro 4000 diesel electric locomotives were ordered from Vossloh. The latest acquisition, for the Jerusalem high speed line, is of Bombardier TRAXX electric locomotives. Siemens Desiro EMUs entered service in Israel in 2019. Passenger trains are formed of Bombardier double deck, Siemens Viaggio single deck and 37 locally assembled Alstom push-pull coaches.

A decades long delay came to an end when the Jerusalem High Speed Railway Project was finally approved and executed, over several years, starting in 2001. The existing line from Tel Aviv was reopened as far as Bet Shemesh station on 13th September 2003, and in April 2005, full service was available again to Jerusalem-Malha station, on the city's southern outskirts. The need for a modern railway, however, was well felt, due to the permanent speed restriction on the tightly-curved section leading up to Jerusalem and the conversion in 2013 of the original station in central Jerusalem to a shopping mall. A new and shorter route was created and formally inaugurated in 2018, calling at Ben Gurion International Airport and with a new underground terminal that was named after Itzhak Navon, Israel's fifth president. The total travel time to Tel Aviv is forty minutes.

The first of two noteworthy railway projects in Israel is the Haifa-Bet Shean line, generally along the western Hedjaz Railway's route. The original narrow gauge line was closed down in the 1950s, and whole track sections were dismantled and carried away as scrap metal. Rehabilitation of the line was considered, but passenger and freight traffic remained insufficient to justify the expense. In 2011, a government decision to link Haifa with Afula and Bet Shean by rail was passed and after five years of work, a single-track, standard gauge line was opened on 16 October 2016 along a modified route.

The second project is the Ashkelon-Beersheba line, which was launched in 2009 and completed in September 2015, with stops in the western Negev communities of Okafim, Netivot and Sderot. Essentially a long suburban line, it was partly built along the same route as the Turkish military railway of World War I and provides an alternative route to Tel Aviv around the Gaza Strip.

Soc.
ANGLO — FRANCO — BELGE

Des Ateliers de
La Croyère, Seneffe et Godarville S.A.

•

*Every type of railway rolling stock
and motive power*

Head Office: La Croyère, Belgium   Cables: Locomoram, La Croyère

ISR diesel locomotive No. 101 (Société Franco-Belge & General Motors, 1951).

Official portrait of Belgian-built Israel State Railways No. 101, the first diesel-electric locomotive delivered to Israel in 1952 by the Société Anglo-Franco-Belge with main parts supplied by General Motors. Two more such locomotives arrived within the same year, marking the end of steam and the switch to diesel traction in Israel. Note the locomotive's elegant Burlington Railroad livery.

A 1950s view of No. 101 hauling seven ex-Palestine Railways wooden coaches on the single track main line between Tel Aviv and Haifa.

A delivery photo of No. 102, seen at ISR's Haifa-Kishon depot.

An official IR colour photo of the new train in Beersheba in the 1950s, with No. 102 at the head of a passenger train from Tel Aviv.

Israel Railways Museum

A wide view of ISR's Lydda workshops in 1959, with a new SAFB diesel engine (101) to the left, four German MF Esslingen diesel trainsets in the middle and finally a new GM/EMD G12 diesel with a Baldwin steam locomotive in the shed. A splendid scene from bygone days in Israel.

A team of Israel Railways workers is posing in front of a new German-built Maschinenfabrik Esslingen diesel train, with the front of Hedjaz Railway 0-6-0T No. 10 (Krauss, 1902) barely visible in the background. Photo taken, probably in Haifa, in the 1950s.

A classic scene from the 1950s in Israel, with a new SAFB diesel engine pulling into Naan station, south of Tel Aviv. Note the original British-built mechanical signalling system still in full use.

Paul Cotterell / Israel Railways Museum

A rare photo of Haifa-East station in the 1950s, with a new Maschinenfabrik Esslingen diesel train to the left and a General Motors class G12 diesel in charge of a Tel Aviv-bound passenger train. The leading coach was built by Orenstein & Koppel.

P class 4-6-0 No. 60 (North British 24219/1935) on the turntable in Haifa.

Making its way to Jerusalem in 1960 in this splendid colour photo is an Israel Railways passenger train, with General Motors (EMD) class G12 diesel locomotive No. 112 (still wearing its original Burlington livery). In the opposite direction, another train is about to pull out of the passing loop and return to the single-track line to Tel Aviv. Note the original British mechanical signalling system still in use at the time and the ex-Palestine Railways wooden coaches - all leftovers inherited in the wake of the British Mandate in this part of the Middle East.

A rare and fascinating colour photo of an Israel Railways passenger train, made of ex-Palestine Railways wooden coaches, here seen at Bney Brack station in the 1950s and possibly on the way to Jerusalem.

A wonderful view of Jerusalem station in 1967, Note the huge "20" on the right side and the "75" more to the left, marking the 75th anniversary of the first railway line in the Holy Land and twenty years since the establishment of the State of Israel.

Ex-Egyptian State Railways class G16 diesel No. 303, taken over by Israel in 1967. It later became Israel Railways No. 163.
Hans Kohut / Israel Railways Museum

A September 1968 picture of Naharia train station, with Car No. 5. This was originally built in Germany in 1956 by Linke-Hofmann-Busch as a driving unit, but was later converted to an ordinary coach before being eventually taken out of service, a few years later. This vehicle is now on public display in northern Tel Aviv.

Possibly the only known photo showing a detailed view of the driver's cab of the Maschinenfabrik Esslingen diesel trains delivered to Israel in the 1950s.

A new Maschinenfabrik Esslingen diesel unit undergoing a pre-delivery test run in Germany.

An unusual perspective of a new German-built Esslingen diesel train, somewhere in the deserts of southern Israel, in 1956. Crew and camel seem to be having a lively conversation!

One of eight new German-built passenger coaches supplied to Israel in 1955 (Nos. 51-58), in an Orenstein & Koppel (Berlin) pre-delivery photo.

A 21st March 1973 view of a Tel Aviv-bound Israel Railways passenger train, shortly after leaving Haifa. ISR diesel No. 111 (General Motors - EMD 24498 / 1958) is at the head of a converted five-car German-built (Maschinenfabrik Esslingen/WMD/LHB) DMU.

Jay Diamond / Israel Railways Museum

A March 1973 view of an Israel Railways passenger train, at Binyamina on the main line between Haifa and Tel Aviv. An ISR class G12 diesel locomotive is at the head of a converted German-built (Maschinenfabrik Esslingen/WMD/LHB) DMU.

Jay Diamond / Israel Railways Museum

Three Israel Railways steam locomotives (ex-Palestine Railways Baldwin 4-6-0 No. 883, LMS class 8F 2-8-0 No. 70503 (North British 24711 / 1941), and another LMS 8F steam locomotive) during a bridge test late in 1954, on the recently completed new main line between Haifa and Tel Aviv. Depicted in this view is the new Yarkon River bridge, in the north of Tel Aviv. Officially inaugurated on November 4th, 1954, the new railway line provided a direct link between the two cities, along the new coastal route. Eucalyptus trees and rich vegetation were once a common sight in this area.

Israel Railways Museum

At an Israeli checkpoint near the Gaza border, Israeli military policemen look at the railway tracks leading from the Gaza Strip into Israel. A portion of the tracks was destroyed in a raid by a band of Arabs on 3rd December 1957. Israel maintained that UN authority in the Strip was on the verge of complete collapse, and continued to press the US to live up to its "moral commitments" in the area.

A new Maschinenfabrik Esslingen diesel train for service in Israel, here seen in Tel Aviv, in an old colourised postcard. Twelve such trains were delivered new to Israel from Germany in 1956.

Israel (ex-Palestine) Railways buffet car No. 504, in a colour slide from the 1950s. It was the first of two Metropolitan Carriage & Wagon Works third class (eighty seats) and BPL coaches built for the Palestine Railways.

On 26 December 1963 two passenger trains on the then single track main line linking Tel Aviv and Haifa collided head-on at Bet Yehoshua station, just south of Natania. The northbound train had passed a red signal and its locomotive rode over and crushed the locomotive of the southbound train. None of the coaches was derailed, but a coupling broke in the northbound train detaching the rear three coaches. The continuous train brake should have then automatically stopped the detached coaches, but it had not been connected properly, so they started to roll back southwards. 55 passengers and crew members were injured in the accident. Fortunately, the two head-end crews survived but their locomotives, ISR Nos. 105 and 118, were completely destroyed and written off.

A pre-delivery colour photo of a new French-built Carel et Fouché passenger coach for service in Israel, seen in Aubevoye, France in 1961.

During the Six Day War of 1967, Israel captured several Egyptian diesel locomotives - ESR Nos. 3304, 3329 and 3361, which were appropriated into Israel Railways stock as numbers 301-303, later 161–163. All have now been withdrawn from service but No. 163 (formerly ESR 3361) is preserved at the Israel Railways Museum in Haifa. Depicted above is one of the ex-Egyptian Railways Co-Co G16 diesels departing El Arish station on the long run to Haifa in 1967. The locomotive is decorated with three (probably four) flags and a large ISR logo between the buffers. The official State of Israel logo is proudly displayed right above that of the railway company. Note the ESR logo below the engineer's side window.

The train to Tel Aviv is ready to depart from Jerusalem station in this 1955 photo of new Orenstein & Koppel coaches.

A Maschinenfabrik Esslingen diesel-hydraulic set inside Lydda Junction maintenance depot in 1956.

An 0-6-0DH built by Maschinenfabrik Esslingen, at Lydda Junction in 1956.

A close-up of the faded Israel Railways logo and running number, 70414, in one of the last known pictures of this former War Department class 8F 2-8-0. 70414 was built by Beyer Peacock in 1940 and survived the war to become the hero of a popular Israeli song from the 1950s about the end of steam in Israel. It was sadly retired and scrapped, but another member of this same class - a Turkish locomotive - is on display in Beersheba, with the same famous running number.

An Israel Railways class 8F steam locomotive with a passenger train, in an ad from the 1950s. The inscription reads, "for your comfort - travel by train!"

No. 101 in an ad from the 1950s. The inscription reads, "Travel by train! (From Haifa) to Tel Aviv North Station in two hours, to Tel Aviv South in 2.25 hours, to Jerusalem in 3.5 hours".

A 1950s view of an Israel Railways train travelling along the Judean Mountains on the Jerusalem line. A neutral corridor was established on both sides of the track, separating the Israeli and Jordanian forces, and providing a safe passage for four trains a day. Interestingly, the short train is made of a new General Motors (EMD) Class G12 locomotive hauling one boxcar and a Southern Railway van, on what could be a test train through hostile territory. The political situation changed dramatically following the Israeli victory in the Six Day War of 1967 and the Jordanian Army's defeat, opening the entire line for uninterrupted traffic.

A 1980s view of downtown Haifa, with a Naharia-bound Israel Railways passenger train pulling out of Bat Galim station, having arrived from Tel Aviv. A General Motors (EMD) Class G12 diesel locomotive is in charge of five passenger coaches. The leading coach is an ex-British Rail type IIc, one of eight bought second-hand in 1977. The back side of a red and white Leyland bus, belonging to the Egged public bus company, is seen on the right.

Still wearing its original Burlington Railroad colours, No. 119 is posing for the camera in front of the station building in Jerusalem. A passenger train, made of dark blue coaches, is partly visible behind the 1954-built General Motors / EMD Class G12 diesel.

A colourful ISR passenger train, with General Motors diesel No. 603 and a set of ex-British Rail coaches, as seen in Haifa on 28th April 1977. It was the inaugural run of the ex-BR coaches in Israel. The coaches only had a/c units fitted starting in 1989 (682 never receiving any) and were withdrawn quite early, around 1997 (except 687 which was damaged earlier in a fire), probably due to their being both non-standard equipment and cracks appearing in their integral bodies. 688 is preserved in the Israel Railways Museum, Haifa.

Israel Railways Museum

No. 120 with a short train made of only three coaches (the leading two are ex-British Rail stock), ready to pull out of Haifa East station on the way to Tel Aviv in 1977. Note the old mechanical signalling system still in use at the time.

Paul Cotterell / Israel Railways Museum

Official General Motors (EMD) works photo of Class G26CW-2 Co-Co diesel No. 613. Fifteen such 2,200 hp locomotives were delivered for service in Israel between 1971 and 1986, this example being delivered in 1984.

New General Motors (EMD) class G12 diesel locomotives being unloaded from the ship that brought them to Israel on May 22nd, 1955.

A passenger train is climbing up the way from Tel Aviv to Jerusalem near Bar Giora, in 1995. In charge of this train is a General Motors (EMD) G12 diesel locomotive, here seen in the attractive colours of the period.

A 1967 view, possibly of El Arish train station, showing an Egyptian State Railways class G12 diesel (General Motors / EMD, 1956) in the wake of the Six Days War and the Israeli takeover of the entire area. Substantial damage to the locomotive is evident in this photo, with what appears to be bullet holes in the driver's cab and the upper body. An Israeli railway official, assisted by several local workers, is assessing the extent of the damage.

Several "Nazi" diesel were captured in North Africa in WWII and were sent up north to Haifa to work as War Department locomotives on the line to Beirut. They remained behind in Israel after 1948 and were unfortunately all scrapped. Here a WR360C14 diesel is being loaded in Tobruk.

A rare photograph of a German-built type WR550D14 0-8-0 diesel locomotive, built by BMAG in 1941/1942, one of three built. It was captured in Tobruk (in the North African desert) in 1943, and became War Department No. 70246. It was then used on the Haifa - Beirut - Tripoli (HBT) Railway. Decommissioned in February 1946 at Haifa East Station and scrapped in 1958. It is seen at Haifa-Kishon Depot.

RAILWAY HERITAGE SITES IN ISRAEL

Looking elegant and in mint condition, Israel State Railways diesel loco No. 101 is drawing attention from two young admirers during the official inauguration ceremony of the new Haifa-Tel Aviv main line on May 14, 1953. This locomotive, the first of three built for Israel in Belgium in 1952, is undergoing a massive overhaul and will soon be put on display at the Israel Railways Museum in Haifa.
Israel Railways Museum

Israel Railways Museum, Haifa

Israel's National Railway Museum was established in March 1983 within Haifa-East station, originally the Hedjaz Railway terminal on the Mediterranean Sea, in downtown Haifa.

Taking home in the old Hedjaz steam locomotive depot and warehouse, the museum is packed with railway relics dating back to the first railway line in the Holy Land, going through the Ottoman Empire and the British Mandate in Palestine, and ending with the Israel State Railways. The museum's archive is rich with original photos and documents detailing every aspect of railway activities in Israel, with a well-kept rolling stock collection both in and outside the vehicle hall. On regular display are Palestine Railways saloon coach No. 98, built by the Birmingham Railway Carriage and Wagon Company in 1922, whose distinguished passengers were Emperor Haile Selassie of Ethiopia, Queen Elisabeth of Belgium and Sir Winston Churchill; Egyptian State Railways coach No. 4720, built in 1893 and used in World War I as a railway ambulance on the Sinai Military Railway; the tender of North British Locomotive Works Palestine Railways P Class steam locomotive No. 62, built in Glasgow in 1935; Israel Railways coaches, including a three car Maschinenfabrik Esslingen diesel train; General Motors (EMD) diesel locomotives; two Belgian-built SAFB diesel locomotives; Esslingen 0-6-0 diesel switcher No. 212; two Cowans Sheldon steam cranes, built in Carlisle in 1918 and in 1950; ex-British Rail coach No. 688 (BR No. M5570) and the highlight of the show, Hedjaz Railway 0-6-0T steam locomotive No. 10, built by Krauss in 1902 and the sole survivor of the many narrow and standard gauge steam locomotives that ever ran in the Land of Israel.

Hedjaz Railway – Beersheba Station

Parked outside Beersheba's Turkish train station is ex-TCDD Class 8F steam locomotive No. 45166 (LMS No. 8267 / War Department No. 341 (North British Locomotive Works, Glasgow 24641 / 1940). It was recovered from Sivas, Turkey in December 2010 by the Churchill 8F Trust and brought to Israel in 2012, where it assumed the identity of Israel Railways No. 70414, another 8F built by Beyer Peacock of Manchester-Gorton in 1940 and the hero of a popular Israeli song from the 1950s, commonly known as "The Locomotive's Song" which is about No. 70414's final voyage from Beersheba to the scrapyard in Haifa, thereby marking the end of steam in Israel. Being a standard gauge locomotive, it had nothing to do with the narrow gauge Hedjaz Railway whatsoever, but it was still placed in Beersheba in the company of a few Palestine Railways coaches.

Hedjaz Railway – Beersheba-Ezuz Line (Negev Desert)

Along the way leading from Beersheba into the Negev desert are the remains of the Hedjaz Railway line to Sinai. A large stone bridge in Beersheba marks the starting point for anyone wishing to trace the remains in the desert as far as Ezuz, close to the border with Egypt, and Nitzana, once a busy railway depot during the attempted Turkish attack on the Suez Canal. The

Australian Light Horse Brigade raided and sabotaged the line in World War I, with track, bridges and stations blown up and completely destroyed, but it is still clearly marked in the sand and a few of the bridges survived and are intact.

Hedjaz Railway – Samach and Gesher Stations (Jordan Valley)
At the southern tip of the Sea of Galilee stands Samach (alternative spelling "Samakh" and in Arabic سمخ) station, on the Hedjaz Railway's extension to Haifa. Inaugurated in May 1906, Samach station originally included a two-level station building, warehouses, a water reservoir made of basalt stones, a locomotive shed and a turntable, with a change of locomotives required for the steep climb from Samach and up the mountains to Deraa Junction, in Syria. A connecting boat service was provided to Tiberias until 1921, when a new road was built around the lake. On 25 September 1918, in a heavy battle, Samach station fell into British and Australian hands, during General Allenby's march on Damascus. Samach then became British Palestine's border checkpoint with French-ruled Syria, and, starting on 21 October 1931, a regular stop on the Imperial Airways service from London via Samach to Baghdad, Bombay and Australia. The station was closed down and abandoned, with the entire western Hedjaz Railway, having suffered considerable damage in Israel's War of Independence in 1948. It was beautifully and thoroughly restored in 2011, complete with the turntable pit, becoming in 2015 a part of the Kinneret College.

Fifteen km to the south of Tiberias, on the way to Bet Shean, is the agricultural community of Gesher (meaning in Hebrew "a bridge") which was founded in 1939 by Jewish German refugees and appropriately named after a Byzantine bridge over the Jordan River, on the ascent to Damascus. It was here that a Hedjaz Railway bridge was built for the same purpose, with a small station that, at –257.5 metres below sea level, was the lowest train station in the world. On 14 May 1948, the Gesher road and railway bridges were sabotaged in a Jewish underground attack intended to cut off the transportation routes from Syria and Jordan into British Palestine, in anticipation of an Arab invasion of the State of Israel upon the end of the British Mandate. Gesher was destroyed during the 1948 war, but was rebuilt a short distance to the west of the site of the original settlement afterwards. In 1992, with the signing of the Israeli-Jordanian peace agreement, a museum was established to commemorate Old Gesher, the railway line and the nearby Naharayim electric power station, which was also evacuated during the war and has been abandoned ever since then. Four Hedjaz Railway freight cars were placed on the railway bridge, on a short piece of the original track leading to the site of the station which was demolished in the 1960s for security reasons.

Hedjaz Railway – Kfar Yehoshua Station
A few miles to the east of Haifa is Kfar Yehoshua, a village afoot the eastern slopes of Mount Carmel and to the south of the historical German colonies of Waldheim and Bethlehem of Galilee. Within the village is Tel a-Shamam train station, which has been converted into a small museum inside the restored Hedjaz Railway station building with an exhibition of railway artifacts and photos.

Haifa-Beirut-Tripoli Railway – Rosh Hanikra Tunnels
Rosh Hanikra (in Hebrew "Head of the Grotto") is where the white limestone cliff of the Ladder of Tyre descends sharply into the Mediterranean Sea, at the Israeli-Lebanese border in the western Galilee. In 1942, as part of the British war effort and the invasion of Syria and Lebanon, a standard gauge military railway was built from Haifa to Beirut and Tripoli, in western Lebanon. The line has since then been sabotaged and abandoned, despite somewhat optimistic postwar plans to extend it all the way to Turkey and Europe. Two railway tunnels were built through the base of the cliff, one of which is now used as a theatre where an audiovisual show is played regularly. The world's shortest and steepest cable car operates between the top and the bottom of the cliff, and a footpath is available to the grotto inside the cliff itself. The track leading into the tunnels was dismantled and replaced with a paved road. A concrete monument, placed between the tunnels, commemorates the completion of the line in World War II.

Jaffa & Jerusalem Railway – Jaffa and Jerusalem Stations
When inaugurated in 1892, Jaffa station was the Jaffa & Jerusalem Railway's outlet to the Mediterranean Sea and the point of departure for passenger trains on the long journey up the Judean hills to Jerusalem. The station was closed down in 1948, sadly falling into a state of decay and neglect, until 2005 when it was thoroughly restored and reopened in 2009 as a lively shopping and entertainment centre under the name "Hatachana" (meaning "the station" in Hebrew). Fashion boutiques, coffee shops and restaurants now reside within the original station building and the adjacent warehouses. Business matters aside, adding to that special atmosphere are a few smart looking Palestine Railways wooden passenger coaches that were placed on a short piece of standard gauge track (the original line was metre gauge), providing visitors with an authentic, hands-on railway history experience.

A similar fate befell Jerusalem's first station, which started life in 1892 as the J & J's terminal outside the Old City walls and right next to Emek Refaim, the historical German Colony in central Jerusalem. The last train departed the station on 14 August 1998. The next day, the station was officially closed, only to re-emerge in May 2013 as a beautifully renovated shopping mall with the catchy title Hatachana Harishona ("The First Station") and with a public park along the railway's route. On static display within the station grounds is Palestine Railways third class passenger coach No. 322, which was built in Britain in 1922 and, after retiring from a long career in Israel, including a military expedition in Sinai in 1956, now doubles as a reminder of the station's heydays as well as space for a model railway layout.

PALESTINE AND ISRAEL RAILWAYS STEAM, DIESEL AND ELECTRIC LOCOMOTIVES & ROLLING STOCK

Detailed in the following list are Jaffa & Jerusalem Railway (metre gauge), and Palestine (PR) and Israel State Railways (ISR) standard gauge steam, diesel and electric locomotives. Industrial and War Department steam locomotives that were used in British Palestine are not mentioned here, nor are the many narrow gauge Hedjaz Railway steam locomotives that were technically under Palestine Railways control, partly remaining in Israel after the end of the British Mandate.

1. Jaffa & Jerusalem Railway (all metre gauge)

No.	Type	Name	Builder	Works No.	Year
1	2-6-0	JAFFA	Baldwin	11011	1890
2	2-6-0	JERUSALEM	Baldwin	11012	1890
3	2-6-0	RAMLEH	Baldwin	11013	1890
4	2-6-0	LYDDA	Baldwin	12585	1892
5	2-6-0	EL SEJED	Baldwin	12586	1892
6	0-4-4-0	BITTIR	Borsig	5464	1904
7	0-4-4-0	DEIR ABAN	Borsig	6682	1908
8	0-4-4-0		Borsig	6683	1908
9	0-4-4-0		Borsig	8970	1914

J & J Mallet locomotive No. 9 was reportedly captured en route to the Middle East, and ended up in Alexandria (Egypt), where it disappeared, having never been assembled.

2. Standard gauge steam locomotives

No.	Type	Class	Builder	Works No.	Year
1-6	2-8-4T	K	Kitson	5360-65	1922
7-12	4-6-2T	H2	BLW/Armstrong	808-13	1926
13-17	4-6-4T	H3	PR		1937
20-21	0-6-0T	USA	Davenport	2417/28	1942
26-29	0-6-0ST	M	Manning Wardle	1937-40	1917
30	0-6-0ST		Manning Wardle	1592	1902
33	0-4-0	RLL	Sentinel	7233	1928
40-46	0-6-0T	N	Nasmyth Wilson	1607-9/23-6	1934/5
47-50	0-6-0T	N	Nasmyth Wilson	1629-30/51-2	1938/8
60-65	4-6-0	P	North British (Glasgow)	24219-24	1935
99	0-6-0ST		Manning Wardle	1492	1900
871-920	4-6-0	H	Baldwin		1918
70305+	2-8-0	8F	War Department		WWII
SC 1-2		RLS	Sentinel (steam railcars)	7432-33	1928
546/50/77	2-6-0	ex-ESR	North British (Glasgow) and Borsig	–	1928
607/13	2-6-0	ex-ESR	all five captured from Egypt in 1956		1931

War Department Class 8F 2-8-0 steam locomotives received from the Trans Iranian Railway after WWII and used in Palestine and Israel

WD No.	Builder	Works No.	Year
305	North British (Glasgow)	24605	1940
308	North British (Glasgow)	24608	1940
335	North British (Glasgow)	24635	1940
336	North British (Glasgow)	24636	1940
369	North British (Glasgow)	24677	1940
374	North British (Glasgow)	24682	1941
388	North British (Glasgow)	24696	1941
391	North British (Glasgow)	24699	1941
397	North British (Glasgow)	24705	1941
400	Beyer Peacock	6980	1940
410	Beyer Peacock	6990	1940
412	Beyer Peacock	6992	1940
414	Beyer Peacock	6994	1940
503	North British (Glasgow)	24711	1941
510	North British (Glasgow)	24717	1941
513	North British (Glasgow)	24721	1941

No.	Builder	Works No.	Year
515	North British (Glasgow)	24723	1941
519	North British (Glasgow)	24727	1941
541	North British (Glasgow)	24734	1942
572	Vulcan Foundry	4718	1936
586	Vulcan Foundry	4724	1936
596	Vulcan Foundry	4719	1936
605	Vulcan Foundry	4763	1936

One more 8F locomotive, No. 70372 (North British Locomotive Works 24680 / 1941), was abandoned in Tul Karm station, off the Palestine Railways Haifa-Lydda main line, following Israel's 1949 armistice agreement with Jordan. It was taken over by Israel in 1967, upon the termination of the Jordanian occupation of Samaria, and was scrapped a few years later.

3. Standard gauge diesel locomotives – Israel State Railways

No.	Type	Builder	Year
101-103	Bo-Bo	SAFB	1952
104-126	G12	GM (EMD)	1955-66
127-130	G12	GM (EMD)	1960-62
131	T44	Kalmar/GM	1989
161-63	G16W	GM (EMD)	1960/61
201-03	0-4-0	Deutz	1953
211-28	0-6-0	MF Esslingen	1956-8
251	G8	GM (EMD)	1956
601-15, 701	G26	GM (EMD)	1971-89
4239	0-6-0	Jung	1955
702-09	JT 42CW	Alstom Prima	1996
731-78	JT 42BW	Alstom Prima	1996-2006
261-63	GA DE900		1997
1301-24	Euro 3200	Vossloh	2011-13
1401-14	Euro 4000	Vossloh	2011

Remarks:
Nos. 127-130, 161-163, 251 and 4239 were ex-Egyptian Railways, captured in Sinai in 1956 (No. 4239) and in 1967.
Nos. 211-228 were diesel hydraulic switchers rated at 650 hp that were similar to the West German Class V 60. When the German manufacturer ceased production, in the 1960s, some of the locomotives were cannibalised due to the lack of spare parts. One locomotive is preserved in Haifa and another, also on static display, is in a public park in Elroy, outside Haifa.
No. 701 is type G26CW-2 delivered to Israel in 1989. Thirteen diesel locomotives of a similar size were ordered from US diesel manufacturer, NRE of Mt. Vernon, Illinois, with eleven that were rebuilt by TŽV Gredelj using parts from Croatian Railways HŽ series 2062 (GT26) units, and two new frames, all designated NGT26CW-3. They were delivered to Israel from August 2015 to December 2017 with the road numbers 710-722.

4. Standard gauge electric locomotives – Israel State Railways

On 30 August 2017, the first new Bombardier Traxx 25 kV 50 Hz AC electric locomotive arrived in Israel from the Port of Bremen for the Tel Aviv-Jerusalem high speed line. The locomotive, No. 3003, weighs 84 tons and is capable of pulling eight double decker coaches at a top speed of 160 km/h. Delivery of all 62 new locomotives is expected to be completed in 2022.

5. Rolling stock – standard gauge DMUs and passenger coaches

No.	Type	Builder	Year	
1-12	DMU	MF Esslingen	1956	
IC3	DMU	ABB Scandia	1992	
51-58		Orenstein & Koppel	1958	
71-84		Carel et Fouché	1961	
91-98		Carel et Fouché	1965	ex-SNCF Inox
111-117		MF Esslingen		ex-DMU coaches
601-643		Boris Kidrič	1961	
681-688		British Rail Mk IIc	1970	
301-305		GEC Alsthom	1996	Push-pull trains
311-342		GEC Alsthom	1996	Push-pull trains
401-		Bombardier	2001	Twindexx double deckers
801-810		Siemens Viaggio Light	2008	Driving Van Trailer (DVT)
825-849		Siemens Viaggio Light	2008	standard coach with wheelchair accessible toilets
901-953		Siemens Viaggio Light	2008	standard coach

31 more SVL units ordered from Siemens in 2010.
Israel Railways have been continuously expanding their already large fleet of double-decker coaches ever since 2001, and are in the process of receiving more such coaches at this time.